4/94

79

CW01080362

Bruce de Mustchine's
ASIAN COOKBOOK

Bruce de Mustchine is a New Zealander who learned the hotel
and catering business from his family. Later in Australia he
produced a radio programme about kitchens and cookery, and
wrote a successful series of cookbooks for Paul Hamlyn
(Australia). He now divides his time between a house in a
Cambridgeshire village and travelling round the world, adding to
his collection of recipes from the different countries he visits.

Bruce de Mustchine's ASIAN COOKBOOK

Illustrated by Tony Richards

NEW ENGLISH LIBRARY/TIMES MIRROR

A New English Library Original Publication, 1981

First NEL Paperback Edition June 1981

NEL Books are published by
New English Library Limited,
Barnard's Inn, Holborn,
London EC1N 2JR.

Typeset by The Yale Press Limited, London SE25
Printed and bound in Great Britain by
Cox & Wyman Ltd, Reading

0 450 05137 4

to
Swami Alakhmurti
wherever you may be
Hari om tat sat

Acknowledgements

In a book of this nature many people assist without them ever realising.
A casual question answered in a Hong Kong market; a tip from a chef in
Japan and long discussions with fellow travellers on board tedious flights
who inform me of likes, dislikes and opinions of different cuisines – all
have helped me to research and compile this book.

To include them all would be a monumental task, but I thank everyone
for such help, for without it, this book may never have been published.
However, there are a few people whose efforts and assistance I wish to
record and to whom my deepest thanks must go.

In particular, the Vietnamese Boat People, both in London and
Australia, who even though they were coping with the problems of
settling in new countries and new environments, had the time and
patience to teach me the methods of cooking from their homeland. Many
thanks.

Bevan Aldridge and the London Walkabout Club must be thanked for
all the travel arrangements they so skilfully made which enabled me to
visit so many countries throughout Asia without any hassles.

Lucy Lo in Hong Kong for her valuable lessons on Chinese cooking;
Henry Chang and the Hong Kong Tourist Association, to you all, thanks
for such an exciting and informative time in Hong Kong.

In Japan, my thanks to Ikuko Nakamura and her friends for an
interesting insight into the Japanese way of life and to Mr Toshiu
Yanagihara for his valuable tuition on the skills of the Japanese cook.

In Singapore, I must thank Mrs Lee Chin Koon, not only for all the
first-hand information on Nonya cooking she was able to give me, but for
the unrelenting energy she exuded to make sure I visited as many hawker
stalls, cooks and restaurants as time would allow.

In London, I must thank with all my heart my good friend and
colleague, Andrew Taylor, whose efforts and assistance needs more than
an acknowledgement in these pages.

I also wish to thank Iwan and Helga Farkas, who so kindly allowed the
use of their beautiful Sydney home for me to complete this book. Also in
Sydney, my thanks to Michael Farkas.

Last of all and by no means least, I thank my dear Ilus, who with the aid
of her Lanier word processor patiently typed the manuscript.

Contents

Introduction

A few years ago, when I was living in Australia, I wrote a book titled *Curries*. The only criticism levelled against that book was simple: that nobody knew who I was. For this, my first cookery book in the United Kingdom, I'll put that right straight away.

For a start, and unlikely as it may seem, my name really *is* Bruce de Mustchine. I was born and brought up in New Zealand: not the most likely place to learn some of the varieties of cooking I've since made my study and my life, but an ideal place to learn the simple, necessary fundamentals of good home cookery. Since then I have had the good fortune to go around the world fifteen times. I am passionately interested in the way different cuisines have evolved: how and why. In this book you'll find not just the ingredients and mechanics of Asian food explained and explored but the historical and social background to a noble food tradition.

Exploring the whys and wherefores of cooking is one of my passions; kitchen simplicity is another.

I've never found it necessary to overcomplicate the preparation of food. Within this book, you'll find that all my recipes – whether from Japan or Malaysia, India or China – can be prepared in the average kitchen, using ingredients from the local supermarket. No fuss. No mystique. But rewarding authenticity.

For starters . . .
The book itself. It's been designed as a cookbook should.

Take any page and you'll first meet *ingredients,* then instructions on *preparation,* and finally instructions on *cooking.* That formula applies to every working page in the book: I hope the other pages are readable enough in their own right!

At the end of the book you'll find some very useful *imperial/metric conversion* charts. After those, a simple *glossary* of ingredients with possible substitutes if you find you can't lay your hands on the right thing at the right time.

Asian cookery

My interest in Asian cookery started with the cuisine of India – and it was fired in the back streets of London. (Sometimes literally!)

Restaurants serving a potpourri of flavours from all parts of the Indian subcontinent were burgeoning everywhere, and I wanted to know how to re-create those fascinating tastes. I read everything I could. I travelled East and was taught by the cooks of India. I soon discovered that my first experiences on the back streets of London bore little relationship to Asian reality. The names of dishes travel a great deal easier than the dishes themselves.

At the same time, I learned that authentic Indian dishes can be cooked in Western kitchens very easily: the ingredients for classic Indian cooking are readily available in the West – if we know what to look for.

I learned something else in India: that my fascination for Asian cookery didn't stop there, but went further, to the cuisines of Indonesia, Malaysia, Singapore, Thailand, Burma, Sri Lanka, Vietnam, Korea, Japan and, of course, China. Part of that discovery has led to this book and, I hope, your enjoyment of some of the great dishes of the Eastern World.

What my book does. And what my book doesn't do

It doesn't cover the whole of Asia and it doesn't give you the whole cuisine of any one country.

It couldn't: Asia is a big, but much more significantly, an old part of the world.

For example, I've had to leave out the cooking of some countries which fall within the Asian definition. The Philippines, Laos, Cambodia, Nepal and New Guinea, all technically Asian, will have to wait for a later book. The Middle and Far East, also: within these pages I come no further West than the Indian subcontinent.

I've also had to compress. Hong Kong and China share a chapter, which may seem mean when you realise that there are as many as 80,000 recorded recipes within mainland China alone, but unavoidable. (For which daunting fact, I'm indebted to my colleague, Lucy Lo, a teacher and writer in the field of Chinese cooking.)

Now you know my book's limitations, consider its possibilities.

I have opened up the 'taste' of the cuisines of the East in a way that you can try for yourself. Wherever I can, I have indicated the origins (or area, or school of cooking) of a particular recipe. That is, I think, important in adding to our pleasure in both cooking and eating Asian food.

Take Japan as an example. Originally the purest of all Asian cuisines, it has, as with all schools of cookery, changed with the influence of history. When Japan began trade with China, oil was introduced for the first time. (Until then, all Japanese cookery had used only water.) Now, with a Westernised Japan a fact of life, Tokyo girls can only eat the dishes their grandmothers cooked by going to expensive 'authentic' restaurants.

Not all outside influence is bad, however. Sometimes, the enforced interaction of two races can create a delightful new cuisine. When the British colonial authorities welcomed Chinese coolie labour into Malaysia, to the Penang settlement, they put the barrier up for Chinese women. Result? Inevitably, Chinese men married Malay women and their offspring became what were known as 'Straits-born Chinese': eventually, the Malay wives overcame their Moslem strictures against the use of pork, their Chinese husbands taught them new methods of cooking, and the wives contributed local produce, particularly chillies and peppers.

The end product of this happy liaison was 'Nonya', a completely new cuisine. Today, Nonya cooking is a splendid blend of Malaysian and Chinese cookery with a hint of Indian spices.

A more familiar example of culinary cross-breeding comes from the British Raj itself. 'Curry' is simply the Tamil word for 'sauce'. To the British incumbents of occupied India, it came to mean a whole way of eating and was, eventually, transported back to Britain. Once there, the ubiquitous 'curry' suffered, mainly from commercial curry powders (unknown in India) and from the use of leftover meats. Even now, few people in Western

Europe realise how easy it is to create a true Indian dish, using fresh meat or fish, herbs and spices, in any reasonably well-equipped kitchen. And that is true for all Asian cookery.

In my chapter on Japanese cookery, I contribute some recipes for very well-known dishes. *Sukiyaki* will probably spring immediately to mind and here it most certainly is. Japanese, but with dubious ancestry! In the late nineteenth century, during the Meiji restoration, the Japanese authorities decided that the populace was eating too little meat protein. 'Eat more meat' was the order of the day. Imaginative cooks – probably with the help of Portuguese traders – created *Sukiyaki,* now thought of as 'the' Japanese dish. I've also included *Chicken teriyaki, yakitori* and *tempura* as being essentially Japanese but acceptable to the Western palate. Raw fish dishes, delicious as they are, I have excluded as being too delicately difficult to prepare unless you can be one hundred per cent sure of your ingredients.

Indonesia and Malaysia share many dishes and cooking methods. In a number of cases, it isn't possible to claim one dish as definitely Indonesian or definitely Malaysian. However, I doubt if you'll care about origins once you start cooking!

Thai food is rated by many experts as the most exciting of all Asian cuisines. It is an assault upon sight, scent and taste: brilliant colours, exotic aromas and piquant sweet/sour tastes. In my chapter on Thai recipes I admit defeat: it isn't easy to get hold of banana flowers, lime leaves or fresh turmeric roots, but I hope you like the variations I've given you.

I've devoted a few pages to the dishes of Burma, Sri Lanka, Vietnam and Korea. A few, only because a book is, perforce, of finite length. No reflection on these exquisite cuisines but, I hope, your appetiser to try them again and discover more about them.

Before we cook . . .
Every recipe in this book has been tested and refined in my own kitchen. Without the resources of the large staffs of most Asian kitchens, I've established my own helpmates and I now recommend them to you.

A *blender* is a must. Even in preparing coconut milk from desiccated coconut, it saves at least one pair of hands. The armoury of any modern, adequate kitchen dispenses with the hours of preparation that Asian cookery could easily demand: ovens, grills, hobs and rotisseries will do the job, however 'un-ethnic' they may sound.

Tandoori food, usually cooked in the famous Indian clay oven, can be convincingly and enjoyably cooked in a hot oven or under a grill, after careful marinating in a yoghurt and spice sauce.

A *wok* is considered by some to be indispensable for authentic Chinese cooking. A deep frying pan and a high heat serve equally well, or even an electric frying pan. Buy Chinese bamboo steamers if you can, from a Chinese store, but if not you'll get equally good results from conventional steamers.

As they say in Indonesia: *Slamat makan!*

It means – wouldn't you know it? – Good eating!

Hong Kong and China

The story of Chinese cooking is a story of geography and of history.

The north of China is a subarctic zone: the south is subtropical. Between the two lay a wide variety of climates, soil, provinces and fiercely independent traditions. (Only recently have communications within China improved to the extent that provinces trade openly with one another.) Basic schools of cooking have evolved over centuries and still retain their integrity.

On to that canvas we have to paint more complications. The rich rice areas of the south have given rise to a rice-based cuisine; those to the north do not use rice to any great extent.

Next, imagine China divided into the four quarters of the compass. To the south, in simple terms, we find Cantonese cooking, the most widely known outside China, and taking its name from the provinces of Kwangtung and neighbouring Kwangsi. To the north, Peking cooking; to the east, Fukien; and to the west, Szechuan. These are the classifications of Chinese cooking I have employed in the pages ahead: they are, of necessity, oversimplified, but they will give you a firm grasp of the reasons for the variety within Chinese food that no British corner-shop or restaurant could ever approach.

Hong Kong is the part of ethnic China most accessible to the Western visitor, and it is indeed a gourmet's paradise. A tiny territory, it contains hundreds and thousands of examples of every regional variation of the Chinese schools of cookery. Produce arrives in Hong Kong, fresh every day, from all over mainland China, via a fast and efficient rail service. From very early morning until late evening, Hong Kong's many street markets are filled with Chinese housewives who cling to the tradition of 'two market trips every day'.

The various schools of Chinese cooking have evolved over 5000 years: consequently, fridges and freezers are very much newcomers. The Chinese have developed highly sophisticated methods of preserving food which are still in use today and can be seen in the street markets of every mainland village, town and city: dried fish, salted and buried eggs (not the apocryphal hundred-year-old eggs), herbs and spices and even snakes, alive, fresh and preserved, used both for cooking and for medicinal properties.

China, of course, is vast: some four million square miles of land. However, much of it is unproductive, which concentrates attention on the cultivatable areas where as many as eight out of ten of the adult population work on the land and a policy of waste not, want not, informs every aspect of their lives. This will help you to understand why chicken and pork, for example, are among the Chinese cooking favourites: poultry and pigs require little land, survive happily on scraps and present little waste in the kitchen.

As well as making the most of limited resources, the Chinese are ancestrally used to coping with bad growing seasons, droughts or floods. Everything goes into the pot. Ducks' webs and chickens' feet are both delicacies in China, while we in the West lack the patience to prepare them. (Interestingly enough, you'd be hard pressed to buy either in Europe: our export-conscious farmers often sell them to China!) But whatever the Chinese cook, their scrupulous attention to the quality of their food is legendary. They find our own indifference to the taste and appearance of our food quite incomprehensible. When times are hard, the Chinese have to eat to live. Conversely, when food is plentiful, they enjoy themselves in living to eat.

I've often been asked which Chinese cuisine is 'the best': the hot, spicy dishes of Szechuan? The many *dim sums* of Canton? The elaborate, classic dishes of Peking?

The answer must be a subjective and personal one. For me, there was an early assumption that the claims made for the absolute excellence of Peking cooking must have foundation. And yet, consider where Peking lies on the map of China. It is in the far north, a subarctic zone crossed by the Great Wall which passes some forty miles from the city. There is no close access to the ocean, no major river nearby. The surrounding provinces grow mainly wheat and cereals. Peking and its surrounding area have, in themselves, produced very little that is remarkable in Chinese cooking.

Here, again, the secret of Peking's pre-eminence in food lies in social history. It has been the imperial city of China for thousands of years: the great cooks from every corner of the country journeyed to Peking to provide the emperor with the very best food. At the imperial command, the freshest, finest ingredients were rushed to the city. And so grew a tradition of cooking that is as famous today as ever it was in the days of the great dynasties of the past.

To answer that question again: which is the best Chinese cooking? Quite simply, the dishes you best enjoy preparing in your kitchen and serving to your family and friends. I hope you enjoy the pages ahead and the discovery of the most exciting and varied cuisine in the world.

Starters and snacks
Steamed pork buns (Canton)

Serves 4-6 Cooking time 20 minutes

½ cup hot water
4 oz (125 g) white sugar
½ oz (15 g) fresh yeast or the
  equivalent in dried yeast
8 oz (250 g) plain flour
2 spring onions

8 oz (250 g) cold roast pork
2 tablespoons cooking oil
2 oz (¼ cup) oyster sauce or tomato
  sauce
1 tablespoon cornflour

Preparation
Dissolve 2 oz of the sugar in hot water, sprinkle in the yeast and
allow it to ferment for 5 minutes. Sift the flour into a bowl. Slowly
pour in the fermented yeast. Mix well, then knead for 10 minutes.
Cover with a damp cloth and leave to rise for 30 minutes. Roll out
on a well-floured board and shape into a roll 2 in (5 cm) in
diameter. Slice into pieces 1 in (2.5 cm) thick. Flatten with your
fingers and set to one side. Finely chop the spring onions and the
roast pork.

Cooking
Heat the oil in a heavy pan or wok and stir-fry the onions for 1
minute, then add the pork, oyster sauce and the remaining sugar.
Stir thoroughly for 2 minutes. Mix the cornflour with a little
water and stir into the mixture in the pan. Continue stirring until
thickened. Remove from the heat and allow to cool. Spoon a little
of the mixture into each piece of dough and fold the edges up to
form a bun. Seal the edges with a little water. Place each bun on a
small circle of greaseproof paper in a steamer over boiling water
for 10 minutes. Serve immediately.

Prawn dumplings (Canton)

Serves 4-6 Cooking time 15 minutes

8 oz (250 g) plain flour
½ cup hot water
8 oz (250 g) cooked peeled prawns
2 spring onions

½ cup bean sprouts (fresh or canned)
2 teaspoons soy sauce
2 teaspoons dry sherry
1 teaspoon sugar

Preparation

Sift the flour into a large mixing bowl. Make a well in the centre and pour in the hot water. Use a spatula and mix the flour and water into a dough. Turn the dough out on to a floured surface and knead for 10 minutes. Return to the bowl when the dough has become smooth and elastic, and cover with a damp cloth. Leave for 30 minutes. In the meantime, finely chop the prawns, spring onions and bean sprouts. Mix together and place in a bowl. Add the soy sauce, sherry and sugar and mix thoroughly.

Roll out the dough until it is as thin as possible. Cut into circles, about 3 in (7.5 cm) in diameter. Place a teaspoon of the mixed filling into the centre of each dough circle. Moisten the edges of the dough with a little water. Fold in half and pleat the edges together. Ensure that all edges are completely sealed.

Cooking

Arrange the dumplings in either a bamboo steamer or a conventional steamer and place over boiling water. Leave to steam for 15 minutes and serve immediately.

Barbecued pork (Fukien)

Serves 4 Cooking time 30 minutes

12 oz (375 g) loin pork or pork fillet	1 tablespoon dry sherry
2 tablespoons sugar	1 teaspoon powdered ginger
½ tablespoon salt	red food colouring
3 tablespoons soy sauce	2 tablespoons clear honey
	2 spring onions

Preparation

Cut the pork into strips about 1½ in (4.5 cm) wide. Lightly score the surface. Mix together the sugar, salt, soy sauce, sherry and ginger. Carefully add the food colouring until the mixture is dark red and then rub this mixture well into the strips of meat and leave for at least 1½ hours. Thread the meat strips on to a metal skewer. Hang in an airy place to dry for about 1 hour. Slice the spring onions. Preheat the oven to 425°F (220°C) or Gas Mark 7.

Cooking

Place the pork on a rotisserie spit and place in the preheated oven. Leave to cook for 25 to 30 minutes. During this cooking, brush with a little of the honey to keep the meat moist. When cooked, remove from the oven, brush with the remaining honey and leave it until it dries slightly. Slice the barbecued pork thinly and serve either hot or cold. Garnish with sliced spring onions.

Cantonese spring rolls (Canton)

Serves 4-6 Cooking time 5 minutes

6 oz (185 g) plain flour
1 egg
1 teaspoon salt
1 cup water
4 oz (125 g) chicken breast meat
1½ teaspoons cornflour
3 oz (90 g) bean sprouts (fresh or canned)
2 dried Chinese mushrooms or equivalent fresh
4 cups cooking oil

or 1 packet of spring roll wrappers. Try to buy these, they are much easier.
2 teaspoons chopped chives
1 tablespoon sugar
½ teaspoon salt
2 teaspoons soy sauce
2 tablespoons chicken stock
pepper to taste

Preparation

If you have to make the spring roll wrappers, sift the flour into a large mixing bowl and make a well in the centre. Break in the egg and add the salt. Mix well and gradually add the water until you have a stiff dough. Remove from the bowl and knead on a floured board for several minutes until the dough is smooth and elastic. Wrap in foil and set to one side. Leave at least 4 hours or preferably overnight. Roll out the dough on a well-floured board until it is ¼ in thick, then cut into 18 square pieces. Take each piece individually and roll out as thinly as possible until you have pieces approximately 6 in (15 cm) square. Cover and put to one side.

Finely shred the chicken breast and sprinkle with the cornflour. Shred the bean sprouts. If you have Chinese mushrooms, soak and shred these before using. If fresh mushrooms are used, simply slice and chop.

Cooking

Heat a little of the oil in a wok or a large heavy frying pan. When the oil is hot, toss in the meat, bean sprouts and mushrooms and stir-fry for 1 minute. Add the chopped chives, sugar, salt, soy sauce, chicken stock and pepper. Mix well and stir-fry until the liquid has evaporated. Remove from the pan and allow to cool before using.

Spoon a small portion of the filling diagonally across each of the wrappers and fold in the two sides to cover the filling. Fold the last flap over and roll up and seal the end with water. Heat the remaining oil in a wok or a deep frying pan until it is very hot. Deep-fry the spring rolls, several at a time, until they are golden brown. This should take about 1½ minutes. Drain thoroughly and serve at once.

Soups
Lettuce and egg soup (Canton)

Serves 4 Cooking time 40 minutes

8 oz (250 g) lean pork	5 cups water
1 in (3 cm) fresh root ginger	2 teaspoons dry sherry
½ lettuce	2 teaspoons salt
2 eggs	

Preparation

Slice the pork very thinly. Chop the ginger coarsely. Shred the lettuce. Beat the eggs.

Cooking

Bring the water to the boil and add the pork and ginger. Leave to simmer for 30 minutes, then add the shredded lettuce and sherry. Stir thoroughly, increase the heat and allow to boil for 5 minutes. At the last minute, add the beaten eggs and salt and stir vigorously. Serve at once.

Beef and egg soup (Peking)

Serves 6 Cooking time 15 minutes

1 teaspoon salt	3 egg whites
5 teaspoons cornflour	4 spring onions
1½ teaspoons bicarbonate of soda	4 cups water
1 tablespoon soy sauce	4 cups chicken stock
6 oz (185 g) minced beef	white pepper

Preparation

Mix together half the salt with 2 teaspoons of the cornflour. Add the bicarbonate of soda, soy sauce and a little water. Toss in the minced beef, mix together and leave to marinate for 20 minutes. Beat the egg whites until they are stiff and put to one side. Shred the spring onions.

Cooking

In a wok or a large deep pan, bring 4 cups of water to the boil. Add the beef and the marinade and parboil. Add the chicken stock and the remaining salt. Leave to simmer for a minute or two. Mix the remaining cornflour with a little water, seasoned with a good dash of white pepper and add to the soup. Stir thoroughly. Add the beaten egg whites and stir once more. Immediately pour the soup into individual serving bowls or a large terrine and garnish with the shredded spring onions.

Crab meat and sweetcorn soup (Canton)

Serves 6 Cooking time 10 minutes

1 tablespoon cornflour	8 oz (250 g) canned whole kernel corn
1 egg white	½ teaspoon powdered ginger
2 cups chicken stock	1 cup crabmeat (fresh or canned)
2 cups water	2 teaspoons dry sherry

Preparation

Mix the cornflour with a little water. Beat the egg white until stiff. Put both to one side.

Cooking

Heat the chicken stock with the 2 cups of water. Bring to the boil and add the corn and powdered ginger. Stir well and leave to simmer for 5 minutes. Add the crabmeat and the sherry, stir well and cook for 3 minutes. Thicken by stirring in gradually the cornflour and water. Remove from the heat. Slowly stir in the beaten egg white and serve immediately.

Sweetcorn and chicken soup (Canton)

Serves 4 Cooking time 45 minutes

2 in (5 cm) fresh root ginger
½ chicken, 1½ lb (750 g)
1 can creamed sweetcorn
1 tablespoon dry sherry

1 egg
1 teaspoon salt
2 teaspoons cornflour

Preparation
Coarsely chop the ginger.

Cooking
Place the chicken in a saucepan. Toss in the ginger and cover with water. Place over a moderate heat and bring to the boil. Reduce the heat and simmer for 30 minutes. Remove the chicken, retain the cooking stock and cut away all the flesh. Remove and discard the bones and skin. Shred all the flesh. In a second saucepan, heat the creamed sweetcorn with some of the cooking stock. Add the shredded chicken and the sherry. Simmer for 5 minutes. Whisk the egg with the salt and then pour into the soup. Stir the soup briskly. Add a little water to the cornflour and add to the soup to thicken as necessary. Serve at once.

Hot and sour soup (Szechuan)

Serves 6 Cooking time 15 minutes

1 small dill pickle
3 large mushrooms
1 can bean curd
1 teaspoon soy sauce
2 tablespoons vinegar

2 tablespoons cornflour
4 oz (125 g) roast pork
4 oz (125 g) bean sprouts
1 can chicken soup

Preparation

Finely chop the dill pickle. Finely slice the mushrooms. Drain and slice the bean curd. Blend together the soy sauce, vinegar and cornflour into a paste. Shred the roast pork. Chop the bean sprouts.

Cooking

Pour the can of chicken soup into a saucepan with the same quantity of water. Bring quickly to the boil and add the chopped dill pickle. Continue to boil for 5 minutes, then add the shredded pork, bean sprouts and mushrooms. Continue to boil for 3 more minutes, then add the bean curd. Add the blended soy sauce, vinegar and cornflour, reduce the heat and stir gently. As soon as the soup begins to thicken, serve.

Prawn soup (Peking)

Serves 6 Cooking time 45 minutes

1 lb (500 g) green prawns	8 oz (250 g) long-grain rice
½ lettuce	salt
15 cups water	

Preparation

Peel and devein the prawns. Wash under cold running water and pat dry. Cut them into small bite-size pieces. Shred the lettuce.

Cooking

Boil the 15 cups of water and add the rice slowly. Boil until the rice is just soft. Add the prawns and continue to boil for 10 minutes. Serve into individual bowls and sprinkle with salt. Cover the surface of each bowl of soup with the shredded lettuce and serve at once.

Seafood

Honeyed prawns (Hong Kong)

Serves 4 Cooking time 10 minutes

1½ lb (750 g) green prawns
2 onions
2 tablespoons chicken stock
1 tablespoon lemon juice

2 teaspoons cornflour
½ teaspoon pepper
½ teaspoon salt
3 tablespoons oil
3 tablespoons clear honey

Preparation

Clean and devein the prawns. Wash under cold running water. Pat dry. Slice the onions. Blend together the chicken stock, lemon juice, cornflour, pepper and salt.

Cooking

Heat the oil in a large heavy pan or wok. Add the prawns and the slice onions. Stir-fry for 4 minutes. Add the honey and continue to stir-fry for 1 minute. Pour in the blended ingredients and stir for a further minute, then serve.

Fried scallops (Fukien)

Serves 6 Cooking time 10 minutes

1 lb (500 g) scallops
2 in (6 cm) fresh root ginger
2 tablespoons dry sherry
2 tablespoons soy sauce
2 eggs

½ cup plain flour
3 tablespoons water
1 teaspoon salt
½ teaspoon pepper
1 lemon
3 cups vegetable oil

Preparation

Wash the scallops under cold running water. Drain and pat dry. Finely grate the ginger and add the sherry and soy sauce. Marinate the scallops in this mixture for 3 minutes. Beat the eggs. Sift the flour into a bowl and add the beaten eggs, water, pepper and salt. Beat together to form a batter. Slice the lemon.

Cooking

Heat the oil in a deep pan. Take the scallops straight from the marinade into the batter, making sure they are well coated, and

then directly into the hot oil. Allow them to fry until they become
golden brown, remove, drain and serve. Garnish with the lemon
slices.

Spicy fried prawns (Szechuan)

Serves 4 Cooking time 8 minutes

1 lb (500 g) large green prawns	1 tablespoon tomato sauce
1 spring onion	1 teaspoon soy sauce
1 in (2.5 cm) fresh root ginger	½ teaspoon salt
2 teaspoons tabasco sauce	5 cups oil
	1 tablespoon dry sherry

Preparation
Peel and devein the prawns. Wash under cold running water. Dry
thoroughly. Mince together the spring onion and the ginger. Mix
together the tabasco sauce, tomato sauce, soy sauce and the salt
and put to one side.

Cooking
Heat the oil in a wok or in a large deep pan. Deep-fry the prawns
until they turn red. Remove and drain thoroughly. Pour away
most of the oil, leaving just enough to sauté. Add the minced
spring onion and ginger to the wok and sauté for 1 minute. Add
the prawns and continue to stir for a further minute. Sprinkle in
the sherry and pour in the sauce mixture. Stir for 1 minute and
serve immediately.

Crispy fried fish (Hong Kong)

Serves 4 Cooking time 10 minutes

1 whole white flesh fish, about 1½ lb (750 g)	½ teaspoon salt
2 tablespoons soy sauce	1 cup chicken stock
1 teaspoon powdered ginger	1 teaspoon cornflour
2 teaspoons sugar	2 spring onions
	7 tablespoons oil

Preparation
Clean and scale the fish. Cut a series of deep lines diagonally
across each side, then cut lines in the opposite direction so as to

form a criss-cross pattern. Mix together half the soy sauce with the powdered ginger and rub into the surface of the fish very gently. Mix together the sugar, salt, chicken stock, cornflour and the remaining soy sauce and put to one side. Finely chop the spring onions and put to one side.

Cooking

Heat a wok or a large deep pan. Add 3 tablespoons of the oil. When hot, add the fish and fry for 3 to 4 minutes, then turn over and add another 3 tablespoons of oil. Continue to fry for another 3 or 4 minutes or until the fish is cooked through. Remove and drain. Place on a warm serving dish and garnish with the chopped spring onions. Discard the oil and wipe the wok clean. Add the remaining oil and return to the heat. Pour in the sauce mixture and bring to the boil. Leave to simmer for 1 minute. Pour over the fish and serve immediately.

Cantonese steamed fish (Canton)

Serves 4 Cooking time 10 minutes

1 whole white flesh fish, about 2 lb (1 kg)	1 cup chicken stock
	1 teaspoon soy sauce
2 spring onions	1 teaspoon dry sherry
2 mushrooms	1 teaspoon cornflour
3 slices bacon	1 teaspoon salt
1 teaspoon powdered ginger	2 teaspoons oil
1 tablespoon bacon fat	

Preparation

Clean and scale the fish. Remove the head if you wish; traditionally this is left on. Wash thoroughly under cold running water. Dry carefully with kitchen paper. Place the spring onions on a plate which will fit your steamer. Place the fish on top. Slice the mushrooms. Remove the rind and chop the bacon. Spread the sliced mushrooms and bacon on top of the fish, then sprinkle with the powdered ginger. Put a few dabs of bacon fat on top and place the plate in a suitable steamer. Mix together the chicken stock, soy sauce, sherry, cornflour and salt.

Cooking

Steam the fish over a very high heat for 7 to 10 minutes. Drain and place on a warm serving plate. In a small pan, heat the oil and add the mixed sauce. Stir and bring to the boil. Pour over the fish and serve immediately.

Fish in tomato sauce (Fukien)

Serves 4 Cooking time 15 minutes

1½ lb (750 g) white fish fillets (cod, snapper)	2 teaspoons soy sauce
	2 teaspoons dry sherry
1 teaspoon salt	1 tablespoon water
3 tablespoons cornflour	3 spring onions
3 tablespoons tomato sauce	2 tablespoons oil

Preparation

Skin the fish fillets. Remove any bones and cut into large bite-size pieces. Sprinkle with the salt, then with 2 tablespoons of corn-flour. Make sure all the fish is completely dusted with the corn-flour. Mix together the tomato sauce, soy sauce, sherry, water and the remaining cornflour. Coarsely chop the spring onions.

Cooking

Heat the oil in a large heavy pan or wok. Add the fish pieces and fry until golden brown. Pour the sauce mixture into a saucepan and quickly bring to the boil. Remove the pieces of fish from the pan, drain and place in the sauce. Reduce the heat and simmer for 2 minutes before pouring into a serving bowl. Garnish with the chopped spring onions.

Braised fish (Canton)

Serves 4 Cooking time 15 minutes

4 large white fish fillets (cod, snapper)	1 cup water
	1 clove garlic
1 teaspoon salt	1 onion
2 teaspoons soy sauce	4 spring onions
1 tablespoon dry sherry	3 teaspoons oyster sauce
1 tablespoon cornflour	

Preparation

Wash the fillets and dry with kitchen paper. Sprinkle with the salt. Mix together the soy sauce, sherry, cornflour and water. Chop the clove of garlic. Coarsely chop the onion. Finely chop the spring onions.

Cooking

Heat the oil in a heavy pan. Add the fish fillets and fry until golden brown on both sides. Remove and drain. Discard most of the oil, leaving just enough to fry the garlic. When the garlic is brown, add the oyster sauce and the chopped onion. Stir for 1 minute, then add the blended sauce. Stir all the ingredients and return the fish fillets to the pan. Simmer for 3 minutes. Place the fish on a serving platter and pour over the sauce. Garnish with the chopped spring onions.

Meat
Steamed spareribs (Szechuan)

Serves 4 Cooking time 1 hour

1 lb (500 g) pork spareribs	1 tablespoon white wine vinegar
3 tablespoons tomato sauce	½ teaspoon sugar
1 tablespoon water	½ cup cornflour
½ teaspoon salt	1 teaspoon chilli powder
1 onion	

Preparation

Cut the spareribs into small pieces with a heavy cleaver. Mix together the tomato sauce, water and salt and marinate the spareribs in this sauce for 1 hour. In the meantime, finely chop the onion and mix it with the vinegar. Add the sugar, 1 tablespoon of cornflour and the chilli powder. Place the rest of the cornflour into a plastic bag. Drain away the excess liquid from the marinated spareribs and tip them into the plastic bag. Shake well to coat each sparerib with cornflour. Spread the onion mixture on a plate and place the spareribs on top.

Cooking

Place the plate in a steamer over boiling water and steam for 1 hour until the meat is tender. Serve immediately.

Szechuan stir-fried lamb (Szechuan)

Serves 4 Cooking time 4 minutes

1 lb (500 g) lean lamb	3 in (7.5 cm) fresh root ginger
3 teaspoons cornflour	2 teaspoons soy sauce
½ teaspoon salt	1 teaspoon sugar
1 clove garlic	2 teaspoons dry sherry
2 spring onions	½ cup oil

Preparation

Slice the lamb into thin bite-size pieces and sprinkle with 1 teaspoon of the cornflour. Sprinkle with the salt. Mix well together. Crush and chop the garlic. Cut the spring onions into 1-in (2.5-cm) pieces. Cut the ginger into small thin strips. Mix together the soy sauce, sugar, sherry and the remaining cornflour. Put to one side.

Cooking

Heat the oil in a wok or a large deep pan until it is very hot. Add the lamb and stir-fry for 1 minute. Remove and put to one side. Discard most of the oil and stir-fry the garlic, ginger and spring onions for ½ minute. Return the meat to the pan and continue to stir-fry for another ½ minute. Pour in the sauce mixture and stir until the sauce is thickened. Serve immediately.

Sweet and sour pork (Peking)

Serves 4 Cooking time 20 minutes

1 lb (500 g) boned lean pork	1 tablespoon sugar
2 eggs	1 tablespoon tomato sauce
4 tablespoons cornflour	4 teaspoons soy sauce
1 green pepper	1 teaspoon white pepper
1 red pepper	1 teaspoon salt
2 onions	2 teaspoons dry sherry
1 small can pineapple pieces	3½ cups oil
2 spring onions	1 clove garlic
2 tablespoons white wine vinegar	

Preparation

Cut the pork into bite-size pieces, trimming away any fat. Beat the eggs together. Cut the red and green peppers in half, remove the seeds and cut into small bite-size pieces. Chop the onions. Open the can of pineapple, drain and retain the juice. Put the peppers, onion and pineapple together in a bowl and set to one side. Coarsely chop the spring onions and put to one side. To the pineapple juice add the vinegar, sugar, tomato sauce, soy sauce, pepper, salt, sherry and 1 teaspoon of cornflour. Blend together thoroughly.

Cooking

Heat 3 cups of oil in a wok or a large pan. Toss the pork into the beaten egg, coat thoroughly and then put the pieces into a bowl containing the remaining 3-4 tablespoons of cornflour. Coat thoroughly, then drop into the hot oil. Deep-fry until golden brown, remove, drain and put to one side. Drain the oil from the wok. Place it back on the heat and add the remaining ½ cup of oil. Crush the garlic and toss into the hot oil. When this is just starting to brown, remove, and add the peppers, onion and pineapple. Stir-fry for 3 minutes, then return the deep-fried pork. Stir-fry together for a further minute. Quickly stir together the sauce, once again, and pour into the wok. Continue to stir until the sauce thickens. Serve immediately, garnished with the chopped spring onions.

Sesame beef (Peking)

Serves 4 Cooking time 8 minutes

8 oz (250 g) cold roast beef	2 tablespoons chicken stock
2 tablespoons sugar	2 cups oil
1 tablespoon soy sauce	1 tablespoon sesame seeds
½ tablespoon dry sherry	

Preparation

Slice the cold roast beef very thinly. Mix together the sugar, soy sauce, sherry and chicken stock.

Cooking

Heat ½ tablespoon of oil in a wok or a large deep pan. When hot, toss in the sesame seeds and stir-fry for 1 minute. Remove by straining and put to one side. Add the remaining oil and allow to get very hot. Deep-fry the beef for ½ minute. Remove and drain. Repeat the process five times or until the beef is very crisp. Discard most of the oil and heat the remainder. Toss in the crisp fried beef and stir-fry for a few seconds, then pour in the mixed sauces. Continue to stir-fry over a moderate heat for 1 or 2 minutes or until the sauce is nice and thick and most of the liquid has evaporated. Transfer to a hot serving dish, sprinkle with the fried sesame seeds and serve immediately.

Mongolian hot pot (Peking)

Serves 6 Cooking time at table

2 lb (1 kg) lean boned shoulder of lamb	4 tablespoons mustard
8 oz (250 g) cabbage	4 tablespoons soy sauce
4 oz (125 g) thin noodles	6 spring onions
4 tablespoons wine vinegar	pepper
4 tablespoons chilli sauce	salt
4 tablespoons tomato sauce	7 cups of good chicken stock

Preparation
Slice the lamb very thinly. Finely shred the cabbage. Soak the noodles in water for at least 1 hour. Pour the vinegar, chilli sauce, tomato sauce, mustard and soy sauce into separate small serving bowls. Chop the spring onions into 1-in (2.5-cm) lengths and place in a small serving bowl. Put the pepper and salt into small open dishes.

Cooking
Heat the chicken stock over a table cooker, i.e. a fondue pot. With chopsticks, each guest dips a piece of the thinly sliced lamb into the boiling chicken stock until it is cooked. It is then dipped into any combination of the sauces and seasonings. When all the meat is eaten, add the shredded cabbage and noodles to the stock, bring to the boil and cook until the noodles are soft. Serve and eat as a soup.

Poultry

Salt chicken (Fukien)

Note: The chicken must be left to hang overnight.

Serves 4 Cooking time 1 hour 10 minutes

1 3-lb (1.5-kg) chicken
7 lb (3½ kg) coarse sea salt

Preparation

Wash and dry the chicken. Hang up to dry overnight.

Cooking

The next day preheat the oven to 400°F, 205°C or Gas Mark 6.
Place the salt in a large flameproof casserole and place in the
preheated oven until the salt is hot. Remove the casserole from
the oven, bury the chicken under the salt and put on the lid.
Reduce the oven temperature to 375°F, 190°C or Gas Mark 5.
Place over a low heat for 10 minutes, then place in the oven for 1
hour. Remove the chicken, cut into small serving pieces and serve
at once.

Crispy fried chicken (Peking)

Serves 4 Cooking time 20 minutes

1 3-lb (1.5-kg) chicken
2 tablespoons dry sherry
2 teaspoons salt
3 teaspoons sugar
½ teaspoon pepper

½ teaspoon 5-spice powder
2 eggs
2 tablespoons cornflour
oil for deep-frying

Preparation

Wash and pat dry the chicken. Rub all over with the sherry, then
the salt and sugar, then the oil and finally with the pepper and
5-spice powder. Beat the eggs and brush on to the chicken.
Sprinkle thickly with the cornflour.

Cooking

Choose a pan large enough to deep-fry the whole chicken. Heat
the oil to smoking point, then carefully lower the chicken into the
pan. Reduce the heat and deep-fry the chicken until it is golden

brown. Lift out and drain thoroughly. Leave to stand for at least 30 minutes. Reheat the oil and replace the chicken. Continue to deep-fry until the chicken is well browned. Drain, cut into serving portions and serve.

Beggar's chicken (Peking)

Serves 6 Cooking time 2¼ hours

6 mushrooms	2 teaspoons oil
2 dill pickles	2 teaspoons soy sauce
1 onion	2 teaspoons dry sherry
8 oz (250 g) fatty pork	2 teaspoons sugar
1 4½-lb (2-kg) chicken	1 teaspoon pepper
3 lb (1.5 kg) plain flour	10 large outer cabbage leaves

Preparation
Chop the mushrooms. Chop the dill pickles. Chop the onion. Dice the pork. Wash and pat dry the chicken. Mix the flour with enough water to make a stiff paste. Preheat the oven to 375°F, 190°C or Gas Mark 5.

Cooking
Heat the oil in a large heavy pan. Put in the diced pork and sauté for 15 minutes. Add the mushrooms, dill pickles and onion and stir-fry for 5 minutes. Add the soy sauce, sherry, sugar and pepper. Stir-fry for a further 5 minutes, then put to one side to cool. Stuff the cavity of the chicken with the stir-fried ingredients. Sew up the cavity. Wrap the chicken in cabbage leaves. Cover with the thick paste, making sure there are no cracks or holes which will allow the juices to escape. Place the encased chicken on a baking sheet in the preheated oven. Bake for 2 hours. When ready, break open the casing and tear away the cabbage leaves before serving.

Walnut chicken (Peking)

Serves 4 Cooking time 20 minutes

4 oz (125 g) shelled walnut halves	1 tablespoon dry sherry
1 teaspoon salt	1 tablespoon cornflour
1 3-lb (1.5 kg) chicken	2 tablespoons oil
6 small mushrooms	1 clove garlic
3 stalks celery	2 tablespoons oyster sauce
1 tablespoon soy sauce	6 spring onions

Preparation

Soak the walnuts in boiling water with half the salt until the skins remove easily, then drain and peel. Disjoint the chicken, remove all the bones and skin and dice the flesh. Slice the mushrooms. Dice the celery. Mix together the soy sauce, sherry, cornflour and the remaining salt. Pour this mixture over the diced chicken and mix well.

Cooking

Heat the oil in a large pan or a wok over a high heat. Fry the clove of garlic until it is golden brown, then discard. Add the chicken mixture to the pan and stir-fry. When the chicken is just cooked, add the walnuts, mushrooms and celery. Continue to stir-fry. Pour in the oyster sauce and stir-fry for 2 minutes. Serve garnished with the spring onions.

Lemon chicken (Canton)

Serves 4 Cooking time 45 minutes

1 clove garlic	2 teaspoons sugar
1 lemon	¼ teaspoon cinnamon powder
2 in (5 cm) fresh root ginger	1 3-lb (1.5-kg) chicken
1 teaspoon soy sauce	juice of 1 lemon
1 teaspoon salt	cornflour to thicken

Preparation

Finely chop the garlic. Slice the lemon very finely. Grate the ginger. Mix together the soy sauce, salt, sugar and cinnamon. Place the chicken in a bowl or deep dish. Place half the sliced lemon on top. Sprinkle with the chopped garlic and the grated ginger. Pour the sauce mixture over the chicken.

Cooking

Place the bowl or dish containing the chicken into a suitable steamer. Steam for 30 minutes, then turn the chicken over and steam for a further 30 minutes. Remove from the steamer and retain all the juices and sauce. Cut the chicken into serving portions and place in a warm oven.

Discard the lemon slices and pour all the juices and sauce into a small saucepan. Add the lemon juice. Mix the cornflour with a little water to a paste and add to the sauce. Place the pan over a moderate heat and stir until the sauce thickens. Serve the pieces of chicken garnished with the remaining slices of lemon and the sauce poured over.

Steamed chicken (Fukien)

Serves 4   Cooking time 45 minutes

1 3-lb (1.5-kg) chicken	1 tablespoon dry sherry
2 teaspoons salt	2 slices lemon
3 in (9 cm) fresh root ginger	

Preparation

Rub both the inside and out of the chicken with the salt. Finely grate the ginger and mix together with the sherry. Spread this mixture over the surface of the chicken.

Cooking

Place the chicken in a suitable steamer and steam over boiling water for 45 minutes or until the chicken is tender. Garnish with the slices of lemon and serve.

Peking duck (Peking)

Serves 4-6   Cooking time 1 hour

1 duck, about 6 lb (3 kg)	2 teaspoons salt
5 tablespoons soy sauce	$\frac{3}{4}$ cup water
1 tablespoon malt vinegar	8 cups oil
3 tablespoons golden syrup	$\frac{1}{2}$ cucumber
1$\frac{1}{4}$ lb (625 g) plain flour	8 spring onions
2 oz (60 g) rice flour	hoisin sauce or plum sauce

Preparation

Thoroughly clean the duck. Pat dry. Mix together the soy sauce, vinegar and golden syrup. Paint the skin of the duck with this mixture and hang to dry in an airy place for approximately 3 hours. Combine the flour, rice flour, salt, water and 1 teaspoon of the oil to make a dough. Roll out the dough until very thin and cut into circles approximately 5 in (15 cm) in diameter. Brush one side of each of the pancakes with a little of the oil, then put two together, oiled side inwards, and stack. Cut the cucumber and spring onions into small matchstick-size pieces. Preheat the oven to 400°F, 205°C or Gas Mark 6.

Cooking

Put the duck in the preheated oven and roast for 35 minutes. While the duck is cooking, heat a heavy frying pan and cook the pancakes in pairs for 1½ minutes on each side or until they puff up and the surface bubbles. Separate the pancakes and stack. Place the pancakes on a plate in a steamer and steam for 5 minutes before serving. In a large pan or wok, heat the remaining oil until it is very hot. Hold the duck above the oil and pour the hot oil over the skin until the duck turns golden brown. Carve the duck into thin slices and arrange the crisp skin pieces and the meat separately. Serve the pancakes with the cucumber, spring onion and sauce.

To eat, spread the pancake with some sauce, add duck pieces and skin, a few pieces of cucumber and onion, roll up tightly and fold over one end. It is left up to the individual diners at the table to make their own pancake rolls.

Szechuan smoked duck (Szechuan)

Note: This must be started at least 28 hours before you plan to serve

Serves 4-6 Cooking time 4 hours

1 duck, about 6 lb (3 kg)	1 cup tealeaves
1 tablespoon freshly ground black peppercorns	1 cup rice
	1 cup sugar
2 teaspoons salt	10 cups oil for deep-frying

Preparation

Clean and remove any excess fat from the duck. Rub the duck all over, inside and out, with the salt and the freshly ground black peppercorns. Wrap the duck in aluminium foil and place it in a refrigerator for 24 hours. Remove, rinse and pat dry.

Cooking

Place the duck in a suitable steamer and steam over boiling water for 1½ hours. In the meantime, line a large wok or deep pan with aluminium foil. Mix together the tealeaves, rice and sugar and sprinkle over the foil. Place a rack on top, so that you can rest the duck about 2 in (5 cm) above the bottom of the wok. Put the steamed duck on its back on the rack and cover with a fitting lid. Dampen two teatowels and place around the edges to stop too much smoke escaping. Place the wok over a high heat – the heat will make the tea smoke and so give the duck its distinctive flavour. Smoke in this fashion for 10 minutes over a high heat, reduce to a low heat and smoke for 20 minutes before removing completely. Leave the duck in the wok until the smoke completely disperses. Remove and leave to cool for about 2 hours. Heat the oil in a wok or a large deep pan and when hot, put in the duck. Spoon the hot oil continuously over the duck for 8 minutes, then remove and drain thoroughly. Garnish with parsley and serve immediately.

Desserts

Cantonese banana pancakes (Canton)

Serves 4 Cooking time 20 minutes

3 tablespoons plain flour	2 very ripe bananas
¼ cup milk	1 egg
pinch salt	2 tablespoons sugar
	butter for frying

Preparation

Blend together the flour, milk and salt. Leave to stand for 15 minutes before using. Mash the bananas, then add the egg and sugar and blend until you have a smooth paste. Mix together the banana mixture and batter and beat thoroughly until all ingredients are blended.

Cooking

Put a small amount of butter into a hot frying pan and let it melt completely. Pour in ⅛ of the blended mixture and fry until golden brown. Turn over and brown the other side. Repeat until you have 8 pancakes. Serve either hot or cold.

Fried custard (Canton)

Serves 6 Cooking time 20 minutes

3 eggs	1 tablespoon sugar
1 cup water	1 teaspoon almond essence
½ cup plain flour	3 tablespoons oil
4 tablespoons cornflour	3 tablespoons caster sugar

Preparation

Beat the eggs together. Add the water, beating continuously. Mix together the flour, 1 tablespoon of the cornflour and the sugar. Make a well in the dry ingredients in a bowl, then pour in the beaten eggs. Stir continuously until your have a smooth lump-free custard. Add the almond essence and pour into a saucepan.

Cooking

Place the saucepan containing the custard over a gentle heat and bring to the boil. Stir constantly until it is nice and thick. Pour into a shallow dish and leave to set. When set, cut into thin strips and sprinkle the remaining cornflour. Heat the oil in a pan and gently fry the strips of custard until golden brown. Drain, sprinkle with the caster sugar and serve at once.

Honey walnuts (Peking)

Serves 6 Cooking time 15 minutes

1 teaspoon salt	3 tablespoons honey
2 cups water	3 teaspoons sugar
8 oz (250 g) shelled walnut halves	2 teaspoons cornflour
	oil for frying

Preparation

Dissolve the salt in the water. Add the walnuts and leave to soak until the skins peel off easily. Blend together the honey and the sugar.

Cooking

Heat the oil in a heavy pan or wok and add the peeled walnuts. Fry until the walnuts are just starting to turn brown. Remove and discard the oil. Return the walnuts to the pan and add the blended honey and sugar. Stir well. Mix the cornflour with a little water and add to the pan. Continue to stir until the mixture thickens, then serve at once.

Almond jelly (Peking)

Serves 6 Cooking time 5 minutes

3 cups water	½ cup evaporated milk
6 teaspoons gelatine	1 teaspoon almond essence
1 cup sugar	1 can mandarin segments

Cooking

Bring the water to the boil and add the gelatine. Stir constantly until the gelatine dissolves, then add the sugar and continue to stir until the sugar has dissolved. Remove from the heat and pour into a flat dish. Pour in the evaporated milk and the almond essence and stir. Leave to set. When firm, cut into small bite-size pieces and arrange in a serving bowl. Garnish with the mandarin segments.

Steamed fruit cake (Peking)

Serves 6-9 Cooking time 30 minutes

5 cooking apples	2 tablespoons shelled walnut
½ teaspoon salt	pieces
1 tablespoon sugar	1 banana
1 cup canned sliced peaches	2 tablespoons blanched almonds
3 tablespoons raisins	

Preparation

Core, peel and slice the apples. Place in a large bowl. Sprinkle with the salt and half the sugar. Add the peaches, raisins and walnuts. Slice the banana and add together with the almonds. Sprinkle with the remaining sugar and mix well. Cover the bowl with aluminium foil.

Cooking

Place in a steamer and steam for 30 minutes, turn out and serve at once.

Toffee apple (Szechuan)

Serves 6 Cooking time 10 minutes

4 firm apples	1 cup golden syrup
4 oz (250 g) self-raising flour	½ cup sesame seeds
4½ cups water	bowl iced water
8 cups oil	

Preparation

Peel, core and slice each apple into 8 pieces. Sift the flour and gradually add 2½ cups of water, stirring continuously. Add 2 teaspoons of the oil to the batter and mix thoroughly. Coat the pieces of apple.

Cooking

Heat the remaining oil in a wok or in a large deep pan. When very hot, drop in the coated apple pieces one at a time and deep-fry until golden brown. Remove and drain on kitchen paper. Drain and rinse the wok and add 2 cups of water. Return to the heat, bring to the boil and add the golden syrup. Stir continously until the golden syrup melts, then remove the wok from the heat. Add the apple fritters and coat thoroughly. Remove and place on a serving plate. Sprinkle with the sesame seeds and serve immediately with a bowl of iced water. Dip each toffeed fritter into the iced water which will turn the soft syrup into brittle toffee. Eat immediately.

India

Food, the ancient wise men of India believe, is 'a gift from the Gods', and its preparation is a form of prayer. Spices are freshly ground daily. Meat and vegetables are combined with spices, fruit, nuts and lentils in a variety of ways resulting in food diverse in colour, texture and taste.

And nowhere will you find 'curry powder' in an Indian kitchen! In fact, you won't even come across the word 'curry'. This is an eighteenth-century British invention which seems to have had its origins in the Tamil word *kahri* which means sauce.

It now adorns thousands of restaurants throughout the world and in particular, England. London alone has 3000 'Curry Houses', which in the main, serve a rather weak selection of Indian dishes. If only a few more would present the cuisine that is truly Indian. The regional variations of Gujarati food, Bengali food, Kashmiri food, Goan food, Punjabi food, Maharashtrian food, Malayali food . . . the list goes on.

The diversity of cooking styles and ingredients is extensive. In the north, the influence of the Mogul emperors and their highly praised Persian cuisine is still in evidence. Rich and lavish dishes of lamb and chicken tossed together with nuts and dried fruits were covered in spicy, creamy sauces and a gossamer-thin sheet of silver or gold. Crisp and tender tandoori food cooked in the charcoal and clay tandoor, minced meat kebabs and the beautiful pilau and biriani can still be enjoyed today in the northern areas of the Punjab and Kashmir.

Centuries before the rule of the Mogul emperors, the Parsis from Iran settled in the western and central areas of India bringing with them their native dishes of *dhansak* and *akuri*, which appear in name only on menu cards throughout the world today. The only way you can enjoy such delicious food is to travel to India or cook it yourself.

The Portuguese Indians of Goa, again, have their own style of cooking. As have the Bengalis to the east, who use a pungent mustard oil to cook the seafood which abounds in the Bay of Bengal and makes up the major part of their diet.

Further south, the coconut palm plays an important part in cooking. Coconut milk blended with spices gives the slightly sweet flavour which is characteristic of the predominantly vegetarian cooking of the area. The southern regions account for most of India's vegetarians. It is here that the fiery hot chillies are used in nearly every dish.

When talking of the vegetarians of India, one must mention the Sacred Cow. To some of us in the West, it may seem irrational that a cow may wander along the streets freely and is not slaughtered for meat. Ask any Indian why and he will tell you that it is the way of his people, the Hindus. Soon you will also discover that the reason why the cow is protected is most advantageous to the country as a whole.

The cow gives milk, which is converted into yoghurt, cheese and sweets. Its dung is the basis of most fires on which food is cooked and it is the beast of burden in the fields. With the lack of agricultural equipment and fuel, India cannot do without the cow. And what is more, in its lifetime, the animal supplies more protein in the form of milk than its body weight could supply as meat. It is, I feel, a wise decree from the ancient Hindu gods that the cow remain sacred.

Over her simple dung and charcoal fire, the Indian cook uses for most of her cooking a *degchi*, a simple deep-sided pot. A heavy cast-iron casserole is more appropriate in our Western kitchens. There is no equivalent for the tandoor oven, but excellent results can be achieved by the use of domestic ovens. A *towa* is used for cooking chapatti and other breads. It is a slightly concave curved griddle, but your heavy cast-iron frying pan is absolutely ideal.

Every meal in India is served with rice and bread. Side dishes of poppadoms, chutneys, pickles, yoghurt mixed with chopped cucumber or onion, Bombay duck, sliced onions, chopped mint and fresh chopped fruit add an exciting variety of flavours to accompany the meats and vegetables. Indians eat with their fingers – you don't have to do the same! But do serve the rice separately and don't make large mountains of food on your plate. Mixing together several different dishes on top of rice and then scattering with numerous side dishes is deemed uncivilised at an Indian table. Have respect for the food that has been prepared. Complex sauces shouldn't be mixed together. Why cook them separately in the first place? Enjoy the food of India.

Starters and snacks

Pakoras
Vegetable fritters

Serves 6 Cooking time 5 minutes

4 cups plain flour
2 teaspoons salt
3 cups water
1 teaspoon turmeric
2 teaspoons ground coriander
1 teaspoon cayenne pepper
4 potatoes
1 green pepper   } or any combination of
2 onions   three or four vegetables
¼ cauliflower
8 cups oil for deep-frying

Preparation
Sift the flour into a large bowl. Add the salt and slowly pour in
the water. Mix thoroughly until you have a thick pouring batter.
Add the turmeric, coriander and cayenne pepper and mix
thoroughly. Dice and parboil the potatoes. Coarsely chop the
onions. Cut the cauliflower into small florets. Remove the seeds
from the green pepper and chop coarsely. Toss all the prepared
vegetables into the batter and mix well.

Cooking
Heat the oil in a deep saucepan. When very hot, spoon in the
batter mixture, 2 or 3 at a time and leave to cook until the fritters
turn a light saffron colour. Remove and drain thoroughly. Serve
at once.

Samosas
Meat pies

Serves 6 Cooking time 35 minutes

10 oz (300 g) plain flour   3 tablespoons vegetable oil
1 teaspoon salt   1 lb (500 g) lean lamb
2½ tablespoons butter   1 onion
1 cup water

3 cloves garlic
2 in (5 cm) fresh root ginger
½ teaspoon turmeric
1 teaspoon garam masala

½ teaspoon freshly ground black pepper
3 tablespoons hot water
8 cups oil for deep-frying

Preparation

Sift the flour into a large mixing bowl. Add the salt and butter. With your fingers, rub the flour into the butter until it looks like breadcrumbs. Add the water and knead for at least 10 minutes. The dough should be soft and smooth. Roll it into one large ball and brush it with some of the vegetable oil. Place it in a large bowl, cover with a damp cloth and leave at room temperature for 1 hour. In the meantime, mince the lamb, onion, garlic and ginger. When the hour is up, break up the large ball of dough into small walnut-size pieces and roll each into a ball. On a floured surface, roll out each ball as thinly as possible, about 4 in (10 cm) in diameter, then cut each circle in half.

Cooking

Heat the remaining vegetable oil in a pan and toss in the minced ingredients. Fry until golden brown, then add the turmeric, garam masala and freshly ground black pepper and stir thoroughly. Add the hot water, reduce the heat and leave to simmer for 20 minutes, stirring occasionally to avoid burning. When most of the liquid has evaporated, remove and allow to cool. Fold each half circle of dough in half so that the straight edges are together. Pinch these edges tight to seal. Now you have cones into which the filling is spooned. Pinch the top together so you have a filled triangular samosa. Heat the oil for deep-frying and cook each samosa, 3 or 4 at a time, for 2 or 3 minutes, or until they are golden brown on all sides. Drain thoroughly and serve immediately.

Soups
Mulligatawny soup

Serves 6 Cooking time 2 hours

1 small chicken	½ teaspoon ground cumin
2 onions	1 teaspoon ground coriander
3 cloves garlic	1 teaspoon turmeric
2 tablespoons vegetable oil	5 cups beef stock
2 tablespoons butter	3 teaspoons salt
½ teaspoon chilli powder	juice of 1 lemon
½ teaspoon powdered ginger	

Preparation
Portion the chicken into about 18 pieces. Slice the onions very finely. Crush and chop the garlic.

Cooking
Heat half the oil in a pan and fry half the onions until golden brown. Set to one side when cooked. In a larger second pan, heat the remaining oil and the butter. When hot, toss in the remaining onions, the garlic and all the spices. Fry for 2 minutes, then add a little boiling water and continue to stir for 5 minutes. Add the chicken pieces and continue to cook until the chicken starts to brown. Pour in the stock and add the salt. Add the first lot of fried onions and clamp on a lid. Bring to the boil, reduce the heat and simmer until the chicken is tender. Add the lemon juice and serve immediately.

Cold yoghurt soup

Serves 4

½ small cucumber	1 cup double cream
10 fresh mint leaves	½ teaspoon salt
2 cups yoghurt	½ teaspoon freshly ground black pepper
	1 cup cold water

Preparation
Grate the cucumber so that you have three-quarters of a cup. Chop the mint leaves very finely. Mix all the ingredients together in a bowl, cover and chill in the refrigerator for 3 hours before serving.

Potato soup

Serves 6 Cooking time 50 minutes

4 large potatoes	2 tablespoons salt
2 tablespoons oil	½ teaspoon cayenne pepper
1 teaspoon cumin seeds	5 cups boiling water
3 tablespoons tomato purée	6 sprigs parsley
½ teaspoon turmeric	

Preparation
Peel and quarter the potatoes.

Cooking
Heat the oil in a deep heavy saucepan. Toss in the cumin seeds and stir briskly. As the cumin seeds begin to fry, add the quartered potatoes, tomato purée, turmeric, salt and cayenne pepper. Stir well and continue to fry for 5 minutes. Pour in the boiling water. Cover and simmer for 45 minutes. Remove from the heat and blend the contents of the saucepan in an electric blender. Serve and garnish with parsley.

Seafood
Grilled prawns

Serves 4 Cooking time 10 minutes

1½ lb (750 g) large peeled green prawns	1 teaspoon salt
3 sprigs mint	2 teaspoons freshly ground black pepper
1 onion	½ teaspoon cayenne pepper
6 cloves garlic	2 teaspoons paprika
3 teaspoons turmeric	2 teaspoons sweet basil
2 tablespoons vinegar	3 tablespoons vegetable oil

Preparation
Thoroughly wash the prawns under cold running water. With a sharp knife prick all over the surface of each prawn. Chop the mint, onion and garlic, then finely mince. Mix these minced ingredients with all the other ingredients thoroughly. Marinate the prawns in this mixture for 8 hours in the refrigerator. Skewer

the prawns on to thin metal or wooden skewers. Baste well with the marinade.

Cooking

Preheat the grill to a medium heat. Place the skewered prawns under the grill and cook for 4 to 5 minutes on each side. Baste 2 to 3 times during the cooking with the remaining marinade. Serve immediately.

Prawn curry

Serves 4 Cooking time 30 minutes

1 lb (500 g) green prawns
2 onions
6 cloves garlic
2 tablespoons vegetable oil
3 tablespoons yoghurt
½ teaspoon chilli powder
1 teaspoon mustard seeds
½ teaspoon turmeric

½ teaspoon ground cumin
½ teaspoon ground fenugreek
1 cup hot water
juice of 1 lemon
½ cup desiccated coconut
2 teaspoons salt
2 sprigs parsley

Preparation

Peel and devein the prawns. Wash under cold running water and pat dry. Chop the onions finely. Crush and chop the garlic finely.

Cooking

Heat the oil in a large pan. Toss in the chopped onions and garlic. Fry until golden brown then add the yoghurt, chilli powder, mustard seeds, turmeric, cumin, fenugreek and the cup of hot water. Stir well and bring to the boil. Reduce the heat and simmer for 10 minutes. Add the prawns and the lemon juice. Cover and continue to simmer for a further 10 minutes. Sprinkle with the desiccated coconut and salt, stir and serve. Garnish with the sprigs of parsley.

Curried crab

Serves 6 Cooking time 25 minutes

3 large green crabs (or several
  smaller ones)
5 onions
4 fresh green chillies
2 tablespoons oil

½ cup coconut milk (see page 105)
juice of 1 lemon
3 teaspoons chilli powder
2 teaspoons salt
1 teaspoon pepper

Preparation
Wash the crabs thoroughly and split into serving portions.
Remove all the inedible pieces. Crack the claws and save the
juices that run out. Slice the onions. Finely chop the green
chillies.

Cooking
Heat the oil in a heavy pan and fry the onions until they are just
starting to brown. Transfer them to a large pan or flameproof
casserole. Add the edible crab portions and pour in the coconut
milk and lemon juice. Add the chilli powder and the chopped
chillies. Season with salt and pepper. Bring to the boil, reduce the
heat and simmer for 20 minutes, then serve.

Fish curry

Serves 4 Cooking time 40 minutes

1 onion
1 apple
2 tablespoons oil
2 teaspoons salt
1 lb (500 g) white fish fillets (cod,
  sole, snapper)
½ teaspoon freshly ground black
  pepper
1 teaspoon turmeric

½ teaspoon chilli powder
½ teaspoon ground cinnamon
½ teaspoon ground cumin
½ teaspoon ground coriander
1 teaspoon flour
½ cup coconut milk (see page 105)
1 tablespoon lemon juice
1 tablespoon desiccated coconut

Preparation
Peel and chop the onion and apple.

Cooking

Heat half the oil in a large heavy pan. Salt the fish fillets and fry them gently until they are cooked. Remove, drain and allow to cool before breaking them up into bite-size pieces. Put to one side. Add the rest of the oil to the pan and toss in the apple and onion. Fry until golden brown. Sprinkle on all the spices and the flour. Pour in the coconut milk, stir well and bring to the boil. Reduce the heat and simmer for 30 minutes. Add the fish, lemon juice, desiccated coconut and stir gently. Do not bring back to the boil. Just allow the fish to heat through, then serve immediately.

Fish steaks in yoghurt

Serves 4 Cooking time 35 minutes

2 lb (1 kg) fish steaks (cod, snapper, jew fish)	1 teaspoon freshly ground black pepper
1 teaspoon turmeric	½ teaspoon cayenne pepper
1 teaspoon salt	1 teaspoon sugar
4 onions	10 tablespoons oil
10 cloves garlic	8 whole cardamom pods
1¼ cups yoghurt	3 2-in (5-cm) cinnamon sticks

Preparation

Wash the fish steaks under cold running water. Remove any scales. Pat dry and sprinkle with the turmeric and salt. Finely chop two of the onions. Quarter the other two and place in an electric blender. Add the garlic, yoghurt, freshly ground black pepper, cayenne pepper, sugar and a little oil. Blend until you have a smooth paste.

Cooking

Heat 8 tablespoons of the remaining oil in a large heavy pan. Add the fish steaks and fry them for 3 or 4 minutes on each side, taking care not to break them up when you turn them over. They should be nicely crisp and brown. Remove them from the pan. Add the rest of the oil to the pan and toss in the finely chopped onions, the cardamom pods and the cinnamon sticks. Fry until the onions just turn brown. Reduce the heat and pour in the blended ingredients. Simmer gently for 10 minutes, stirring occasionally.

Remove the cinnamon sticks and the cardamom pods and discard them. Remove half the sauce from the pan and put to one side. Spread the remaining sauce over the pan and place the fish steaks on top. Pour the remaining sauce evenly on top. Cover the pan and continue to simmer for 10 minutes or until the fish is heated right through. Serve at once.

Meat
Beef madras

Serves 6 Cooking time 2 hours

1 lb (500 g) braising steak	½ teaspoon freshly ground black
3 potatoes	pepper
3 onions	½ teaspoon powdered ginger
3 cloves garlic	1 can peeled tomatoes
1 tablespoon oil	1 tablespoon tomato paste
1 teaspoon chilli powder	2 cups water
1 teaspoon ground coriander	2 teaspoons salt
½ teaspoon ground cumin	juice of 1 lemon
1 teaspoon ground turmeric	

Preparation
Cut the steak into bite-size pieces. Peel and dice the potatoes. Slice the onions and chop the garlic.

Cooking
Heat the oil in a heavy deep pan. Add the onions and garlic and fry for 5 minutes. Toss in all the spices and stir-fry for 5 minutes. Add the steak and stir. Fry for a further 10 minutes. Add the can of peeled tomatoes, tomato paste and the 2 cups of water. Cover, bring to the boil, reduce the heat and simmer for 1 hour. Add the diced potatoes, cover and continue to simmer for another 30 minutes. By this time the meat should be tender, the potatoes cooked and the gravy rich and thick. Season further with the salt and lemon juice. Stir well, then serve immediately.

Bhoona goast

Serves 6 Cooking time 1½ hours

1 onion	½ teaspoon ground cumin
6 cloves garlic	½ teaspoon freshly ground black
2 fresh green chillies	pepper
3 lb (1.5 kg) boned lean lamb	1 teaspoon chilli powder
1 tablespoon vegetable oil	1 teaspoon ground mace
1 teaspoon turmeric	1 tablespoon malt vinegar
1 teaspoon ground coriander	2 teaspoons salt
¼ teaspoon ground cloves	1 tablespoon desiccated coconut

Preparation

Chop the onion and the garlic very finely. Slice the green chillies.
Cut the lamb into bite-size pieces, discarding any excess fat.

Cooking

Heat the vegetable oil in a large deep pan and fry the onion,
garlic and the sliced chillies for about 3 minutes. Add all the
spices, stir well and leave for 5 minutes on a gentle heat. Toss in
the lamb. Add the vinegar and salt. Bring quickly to the boil,
reduce the heat, cover and leave to simmer for about 1¼ hours.
Stir occasionally. When the lamb is tender, add the desiccated
coconut, stir well and serve immediately.

Lamb korma

Serves 6 Cooking time 1 hour

3 tablespoons blanched almonds	6 cardamom pods
3 tablespoons raisins	4 tablespoons vegetable oil
pinch of saffron	1 tablespoon ground coriander
1½ lb (750 g) lean lamb	2-in (5-cm) cinnamon stick
4 small onions	½ teaspoon ground mace
2 in (5 cm) fresh root ginger	2 teaspoons salt
	6 egg whites

Preparation

Place the almonds and raisins in a bowl. Add the pinch of saffron
and cover with hot water. Put to one side for 3 hours. Slice one
quarter of the meat into large thin slices. Cut the rest into
bite-size pieces. Finely slice the onions and grate the root ginger.
Crack the cardamom pods partly open.

Cooking

Heat half the oil in a heavy pan and fry all the meat for 2 minutes. Add the sliced onions, grated ginger and the coriander. Continue to fry until the lamb is browned. Remove all the sliced meat and place in a warm oven. Cover the remaining lamb with water and simmer for about 20 minutes. Remove the meat and place in the warm oven. Retain the cooking liquid. Increase the heat and reduce the liquid by half. Strain and put to one side. Pour the remaining oil in the pan and heat. Splinter the cinnamon stick into the hot oil and add the cracked cardamom pods. Return the pieces of meat (not the slices) to the pan, cover tightly, shake the pan thoroughly and then place it on a low heat for 2 minutes. Add the ground mace and repeat the process. Add the salt and a little of the strained cooking liquid. Continue to simmer until it is almost dry. Quickly beat the egg whites until they are frothy but not stiff. Pour on top of the meat. Add the slices of meat and cook over a moderate heat. As the egg whites set, drain the almonds and raisins and sprinkle on top. Cover and leave on a moderate heat for 2 minutes, then serve immediately.

Beef kheema

Serves 4 Cooking time 45 minutes

4 large onions	1 teaspoon turmeric
4 cloves garlic	1 teaspoon chilli powder
2 in (5 cm) fresh root ginger	1 teaspoon ground coriander
1 can peeled tomatoes	1½ lb (750 g) minced beef
4 tablespoons vegetable oil	2 teaspoons salt

Preparation

Finely slice the onions. Crush and chop the garlic. Grate the ginger. Chop the tomatoes.

Cooking

Heat the oil in a heavy frying pan. When hot, add the onions, garlic and grated ginger. Fry for about 10 minutes or until the onions are just turning brown, stirring frequently. Add the turmeric, chilli powder and ground coriander. Stir well and continue to fry for 2 minutes, then add the meat. Continue to fry, stirring occasionally for 10 minutes. Add the salt and tomatoes and bring to the boil. Reduce the heat, cover the pan and allow to simmer for 10 minutes. Uncover and continue to cook for 3 or 4 minutes to allow some of the liquid to evaporate. Serve at once.

Curried kidneys

Serves 4 Cooking time 25 minutes

1 lb (500 g) lamb kidneys	¼ teaspoon cayenne pepper
1 tablespoon wine vinegar	1 bayleaf
2 onions	2 cups canned peeled tomatoes
3 tablespoons vegetable oil	2 teaspoons salt
1 teaspoon turmeric	½ teaspoon ground mace
½ teaspoon ground coriander	1 tablespoon sesame seeds

Preparation
Put the vinegar in a bowl of water, add the kidneys and soak for 2 hours. Finely chop the onions.

Cooking
Heat the oil in a large heavy pan and fry the chopped onions until just turning brown. Add the turmeric, coriander and cayenne pepper. Stir for a few moments. Drain the kidneys, cut in half and add them to the pan. Fry for 5 minutes. Crush the bayleaf to a powder and add to the pan along with the tomatoes, salt and mace. Continue to fry until the curry is dry, stir regularly and do not let it burn. Pour in enough water to just cover the kidneys and bring to the boil. Cover and simmer until the kidneys are tender. Arrange the kidneys on a hot serving dish, pour over the curry sauce and sprinkle with the sesame seeds. Serve immediately.

Pork vindaloo

Note: This needs to marinate 24 hours before cooking.

Serves 6 Cooking time 1¾ hours

2 lb (1 kg) lean pork pieces	½ teaspoon ground cardamom
1 teaspoon chilli powder	3 cloves garlic
1½ tablespoons ground cinnamon	5 tablespoons malt vinegar
1 tablespoon ground ginger	5 tablespoons oil
½ teaspoon ground cumin	10 peppercorns
½ teaspoon ground cloves	3 bay leaves

Preparation

Cut the pork into bite-size pieces. Mix all the spices together. Crush and finely chop the garlic and add to the spices with the vinegar. Mix well until you have a thick paste. Add the pork, stir well and leave to marinate for 24 hours in the refrigerator.

Cooking

Heat the oil in a large heavy pan. Add the meat and marinade. Toss in the peppercorns and bay leaves. Allow to simmer gently for 1¾ hours or until the pork is tender. If the sauce starts to dry out, add a little boiling water. Remove the bay leaves and serve.

Rogha josh

Serves 4 Cooking time 1¾ hours

2 lbs (1 kg) lamb	½ teaspoon freshly ground black pepper
½ teaspoon cayenne pepper	
1 teaspoon salt	½ teaspoon turmeric
2 in (5 cm) fresh root ginger	4 cups boiling water
2 cups yoghurt	½ teaspoon ground coriander
1 tablespoon oil	½ teaspoon garam masala
2 tablespoons butter	½ teaspoon grated nutmeg

Preparation

Cut the lamb into bite-size pieces and place in a large bowl. Sprinkle with the cayenne pepper and salt. Finely chop the ginger and mix with the yoghurt. Pour over the lamb and mix well. Cover the bowl with foil and place in the refrigerator for 3 hours.

Cooking

Heat the oil and butter in a large heavy pan. Add the freshly ground black pepper and turmeric. Pour in the lamb and yoghurt mixture and stir continuously until it comes to the boil. Reduce the heat, cover and leave to simmer for 1 hour. Do not remove the lid during this period. When the hour is up, uncover and add 2 cups of boiling water. Sprinkle with the coriander and continue to simmer for a further 15 minutes. Add the remaining 2 cups of boiling water and continue to simmer for a further 15 minutes or so or until the lamb is tender. Remove and pour into a serving dish. Sprinkle with the garam masala and nutmeg, then serve.

Koftas
Meatballs

Serves 6 Cooking time 45 minutes

2 lb (1 kg) finely minced beef	juice of 2 lemons
2 teaspoons salt	1 cup oil
1 teaspoon freshly ground black pepper	2-in (5-cm) cinnamon stick
	4 whole cardamom pods
2 tablespoons garam masala	6 whole black peppercorns
1 teaspoon ground coriander	4 whole cloves
4 teaspoons ground cumin	1 teaspoon turmeric
2 fresh green chillies	1 can peeled tomatoes
8 cloves garlic	1½ cups water
3 in (7.5 cm) fresh root ginger	1 tablespoon paprika
6 spring onions	6 sprigs parsley
5 medium onions	

Preparation

Mix together the minced beef with 1 teaspoon of salt, ½ teaspoon of freshly ground black pepper, 1 tablespoon garam masala, ½ teaspoon of ground coriander and ½ teaspoon cumin. Put to one side.

For the stuffing, finely mince the chillies, 2 of the cloves of garlic, half the root ginger, the 6 spring onions and 1 of the onions. Add to these ingredients the lemon juice and ½ teaspoon freshly ground black pepper. Mix throughly.

Finely slice the remaining onions. Chop the rest of the garlic and ginger. In an electric blender blend the onions, garlic and ginger with a little water into a paste.

Scoop up enough of the minced meat mixture to make a ball about 1½ in (6 cm) in diameter. With your finger make a hole in the centre of each ball and fill with a little of the stuffing. Cover the stuffing by bringing the edges of the ball together and making a ball once again. Make up all the meat in this fashion. You should make about 40 meatballs.

Cooking
Heat half the oil in a large heavy pan. Add the cinnamon stick, cardamom pods, peppercorns and cloves. Stir and fry all together for 20 seconds, then add a few of the meatballs. Brown them on all sides quickly, then remove and drain. Continue the process until all are browned.

Remove all the spices from the oil. Pour the oil into a large heavy flameproof casserole and add the remaining oil. Place over a moderate heat and pour in the blended paste of onions, garlic and ginger. Fry for 10 minutes, then add the remaining coriander, cumin and the turmeric. Stir to keep from burning for 5 minutes. Add the can of peeled tomatoes and leave to simmer for 5 minutes.

Add the 1½ cups of water and the meatballs together with the paprika, the remaining garam masala and salt. Bring to the boil, stirring gently. Reduce the temperature, cover and simmer slowly for 30 minutes.

To serve, carefully lift the koftas out of the sauce with a slotted spoon, place on a serving dish and pour over the sauce. Garnish with sprigs of parsley.

Poultry

Tandoori chicken

Note: This should be started at least 14 hours before required.

Serves 4 Cooking time 1 hour

1 3-lb (1.5-kg) chicken
2 teaspoons salt
½ teaspoon turmeric
8 cloves garlic
1 tablespoon wine vinegar
1 cup canned sliced peaches
2 tablespoons mustard seeds
2 onions
3 green chillies
2 teaspoons ground fenugreek
1 teaspoon cumin seeds

4 tablespoons whipped cream
4 tablespoons yoghurt
juice of 1 lemon
3 tablespoons butter
1 in (2.5 cm) fresh root ginger
4 tablespoons chopped chives
½ tablespoon water
1 bayleaf
1 teaspoon black peppercorns
½ teaspoon ground dill
1 teaspoon ground cinnamon

Preparation

Wash and dry the chicken. Pierce the flesh all over with the point
of a sharp knife. Ideally the chicken should be cooked on a
rotisserie spit, so if you are using one, skewer the chicken now for
ease of handling. Rub the chicken inside and out firstly with half
the salt, then the turmeric. Leave for 1 hour. Mince the garlic and
mix it with the vinegar and remaining salt. Rub this mixture into
the flesh of the chicken. Purée the peaches in a blender or pass
through a sieve. Pound the mustard seeds and mix with the
puréed peaches. Mince the onions and green chillies and add to
the mixture along with the ground fenugreek and cumin seeds.
Mix thoroughly together until you have a thick paste. Rub this
paste thoroughly into the flesh of the chicken and leave to
marinate for at least 12 hours, covered, in a refrigerator.

Cooking

When you are ready to cook your chicken, preheat the oven to
425°F, 220°C or Gas Mark 7. Blend together the whipped cream,
yoghurt and lemon juice. Melt the butter and grate the ginger
and add these to the cream sauce. Place the skewered chicken on
the rotisserie or on a baking rack in a baking tray and place in the
preheated oven. Baste the chicken with the cream sauce to start
and then every 10 minutes for about 50 minutes. In the
meantime, pound the chives together with about ½ tablespoon of

water, add the bay leaf and continue to pound for a few seconds, then put to one side. Freshly grind the black peppercorns and add the dill and cinnamon. Mix together, then add the strained liquid from the pounded chives and bay leaves to form a paste. Rub or brush this paste over the cooked chicken and raise the heat to 450°F, 235°C or Gas Mark 8 and continue to cook until this second paste forms a crust. Scrape together all the juices and cream sauce which have gathered on the baking tray and give the chicken one final basting. Remove, carve and serve immediately.

Dry chicken curry

Serves 4 Cooking time 45 minutes

1 3-lb (1.5-kg) chicken	1 teaspoon black pepper
4 onions	2 teaspoons salt
3 cloves garlic	2 teaspoons butter
½ teaspoon ground cumin	2 teaspoons wine vinegar
1 teaspoon ground coriander	1 tablespoon tomato paste
¼ teaspoon ground turmeric	juice of 1 lemon
½ teaspoon powdered ginger	2 tablespoons desiccated coconut
¼ teaspoon chilli powder	

Preparation
Joint the chicken. Slice the onions very finely. Crush and chop the garlic. Mix together all the spices, salt, butter and vinegar. Blend thoroughly and put to one side.

Cooking
Heat the oil in a large heavy pan. When hot, add the onions and garlic and fry for 5 minutes, then remove. Mix the onions and garlic with the spice paste, add the tomato paste and return to the pan. Continue to cook for 5 minutes before tossing in the chicken pieces. Stir well so that the curry paste covers all the chicken. Cover and leave to simmer gently until the chicken is tender. Uncover and check to make sure the chicken is not burning. If it looks as if it might, add a little water. When the chicken is cooked and tender, add the lemon juice and desiccated coconut, stir well and cook for a further 1 or 2 minutes before serving.

Green bean and duck curry

Serves 4 Cooking time 1 hour 20 minutes

1 4-lb (2-kg) duck	1 teaspoon ground coriander
2 large onions	1 teaspoon ground cumin
6 cloves garlic	½ teaspoon chilli powder
1 can peeled tomatoes	½ teaspoon powdered ginger
8 oz (250 g) green beans	½ teaspoon ground cinnamon
1 tablespoon turmeric	2 cups water
2 tablespoons oil	juice of 1 lemon

Preparation
Cut the duck into serving portions and prick the skin all over with
a sharp knife. Slice the onions very finely. Crush and chop the
garlic. Chop the tomatoes. Slice the green beans. Preheat the
oven to very hot, 450°F, 235°C or Gas Mark 8.

Cooking
Place the duck portions on a rack in the preheated oven and cook
for 20 minutes. This will allow for some of the fat to melt and
escape. Remove from the oven and drain thoroughly. Dust with
half the turmeric. Heat the oil in a large heavy pan. Fry the
onions and garlic until they are golden brown. Add the remaining
turmeric along with all the other spices. Continue to fry for 5
minutes, then add the chopped peeled tomatoes. Add the water,
stir well and bring back to the simmer. Add the duck pieces,
cover and cook until the duck is tender. Add the green beans and
simmer, uncovered, for a further 15 minutes. Sprinkle with the
salt and add the lemon juice. Stir well and serve.

Chicken biriani

Serves 6 Cooking time 1 hour

6 onions	1 teaspoon ground coriander
4 cloves garlic	1 teaspoon poppy seeds
2 in (5 cm) fresh root ginger	1 teaspoon cumin seeds
8 whole cloves	5 teaspoons salt
12 whole black peppercorns	juice of 2 lemons
1 teaspoon ground cardamom	1½ cups yoghurt
½ teaspoon ground cinnamon	1 4-lb (2-kg) chicken

1 teaspoon ground saffron	2 bay leaves
2 tablespoons milk	1 cup raisins
5 pints (12½ cups) water	1 cup blanched almonds
12 oz (375 g) long grain rice	3 eggs
4 tablespoons oil	

Preparation

Peel and chop 3 onions. Place in an electric blender with the garlic, ginger, cloves, black peppercorns, ground cardamoms, cinnamon, coriander, poppy seeds, cumin, 2 teaspoons of salt and the lemon juice. Blend together until you have a smooth paste. Pour into a large bowl and add the yoghurt. Stir thoroughly. Disjoint the chicken and remove the skin. Cut into serving portions. Prick the surfaces of each piece of chicken. Toss all the pieces into the marinade, stir well, cover and refrigerate for 2 hours. Stir once or twice while marinating. Slice the remaining onions and put to one side.

Cooking

When the chicken has finished marinating, remove from the refrigerator and pour all the contents into a large pan. Bring gently to the boil, cover, reduce the heat and simmer for 15 minutes. Remove the pieces of chicken with a slotted spoon, and place in a large casserole. Put to one side. Continue to boil the marinade and reduce to about 4 cups. Pour this over the chicken pieces.

Preheat the oven to 300°F, 150°C or Gas Mark 2. Add the saffron to the milk.

Bring the water to the boil. Add the rice and 3 teaspoons of salt. Bring back to the boil and cook for 5 minutes. Drain and place on top of the chicken in the casserole. Pour over the milk and saffron. Pour half of the oil over the rice. Crush and sprinkle the bay leaves on top. Cover the casserole with aluminium foil, put on the lid and place in the oven for 1 hour.

In the meantime, fry the remaining sliced onions in the remaining oil until they are golden brown. Remove with a slotted spoon and drain. Retain the oil in the pan and fry the raisins for 3 or 4 minutes. Drain and put to one side. Hardboil the eggs, peel and quarter them.

To serve, spoon the rice on to a large platter, put the chicken pieces on top, spoon the juices and sauces over and garnish with the fried onions, raisins, blanched almonds and quartered hardboiled eggs.

Vegetables, rice and chutneys
Pilau rice

Serves 6 Cooking time 30 minutes

4 cardamom pods	3 onions
4 cloves	3 cups water
3-in (7.5-cm) cinnamon stick	1 oz (30 g) bacon fat
8 black peppercorns	4 oz (125 g) long-grain rice
1 lb (500 g) braising steak	2 teaspoons salt
1 lb (500 g) lean pork	1 cup milk

Preparation
Remove the cardamom seeds from their pods. Tie them up with the cloves, cinnamon stick (which can be broken) and the peppercorns in a piece of butter muslin. Cut up the steak into bite-size pieces, removing any excess fat. Do exactly the same with the pork. Slice the onions very finely.

Cooking
Put the water in a saucepan and place over a high heat. Add the bag containing the spices and bring to the boil. Toss in the steak and pork and boil until the meat is tender. In a separate pan, heat the bacon fat and fry the sliced onions until brown. Add the rice and continue to fry for 10 minutes. Add the salt and stir throughly. Strain the meat and retain the liquid, discarding the muslin bag. Add the meat to the pan containing the rice and stir for 2 minutes. Pour in the retained meat liquid and add the milk. Reduce the heat and continue to cook until the rice is tender. If the mixture looks like burning, add a little more liquid; an equal mixture of milk and water is best. Serve the moment the rice is cooked.

Coconut rice

Serves 6 Cooking time 40 minutes

1 onion	2 cups long-grain rice
6 tablespoons desiccated coconut	2 cups boiling water
3 tablespoons butter	3 cups coconut milk (see page 105)
salt	

Preparation
Finely chop the onion. Toast the desiccated coconut in a hot oven until it is golden brown.

Cooking
Heat the butter in a deep heavy flameproof casserole and add the onion. Fry for 2 minutes, then add the salt and rice. Fry for a further 5 minutes, stirring continuously. Do not let the rice brown. Add the boiling water and increase the heat. When it reaches boiling point again, reduce the heat and cook for 5 minutes, then add the coconut milk. Bring back to the boil once more, then reduce the heat to as low as possible, but enough to retain simmering. Cover the casserole with kitchen foil and crimp the edges. Replace the lid and leave to simmer for 25 minutes by which time all the liquid should be absorbed and the rice light and fluffy. Sprinkle with the toasted coconut and serve at once.

Mushroom curry

Serves 6 Cooking time 30 minutes

3 onions	1 cup yoghurt
12 oz (750 g) mushrooms	2 cups vegetable stock
1 tablespoon butter	2 teaspoons salt
1 tablespoon tomato paste	½ teaspoon freshly ground black
1 teaspoon ground cumin	pepper
½ teaspoon ground cloves	½ teaspoon chilli powder
1 tablespoon hot water	

Preparation
Finely chop the onions. Peel and slice the mushrooms.

Cooking

In a large heavy pan, melt the butter and toss in the onions. Fry
until golden brown. Add the tomato paste, cumin and cloves. Stir
for 4 or 5 minutes. Add the mushrooms and the hot water.
Continue to cook for a further 5 minutes, then add the yoghurt,
vegetable stock, salt, pepper and chilli powder. Stir well and
simmer for 15 minutes, then serve.

Stuffed aubergine

Serves 4 Cooking time 45 minutes

1 cup mixed cooked vegetables	1 tablespoon butter
(potatoes, onions, celery, carrots,	2 teaspoons ground coriander
etc)	2 teaspoons ground cumin
2 large aubergines	½ teaspoon ground cardamom
1 onion	4 cloves
3 cloves garlic	½ teaspoon powdered ginger
3 green chillies	2 teaspoons salt

Preparation

Chop all the mixed vegetables. Cut the aubergines in half
lengthways and scoop out the centres. Retain the skins. Finely
chop the onion. Crush and chop the garlic. Finely slice the green
chillies.

Cooking

Simmer the aubergine centres in water until soft, then drain,
chop and mix with the vegetables. Heat the butter in a heavy pan
and toss in the onions, garlic and chillies. Fry until the onions
turn golden brown. Add the coriander, cumin, cardamom, cloves
and ginger. Continue to fry for a few minutes, then add the mixed
vegetables and aubergines. Add the salt and mix thoroughly.

Stuff each half of the aubergines with this cooked mixture.
Place in a steamer and steam for about 20 minutes or until
completely tender. Serve immediately.

Pyazwale sookhe aloo
Fried potatoes and onion

Serves 6 Cooking time 35 minutes

1 large onion	2 tablespoons salt
6 potatoes	1 tablespoon garam masala
1 red pepper	juice of 1 lemon
½ teaspoon cumin seeds	sprig parsley
½ teaspoon mustard seeds	

Preparation
Peel and coarsely chop the onion. Peel and halve the potatoes. Seed and finely chop the red pepper.

Cooking
Boil the potatoes until soft. Drain and mash. Heat the oil in a large heavy pan. Toss in the cumin and mustard seeds. Fry for 1 minute, then add the chopped pepper. Continue to fry for a further minute, then add the onion. Cook all together for 5 minutes, then add the mashed potatoes, salt, garam masala and lemon juice. Stir-fry for 7 minutes. Serve garnished with the parsley.

Fruit chutney
Makes enough for several curries Cooking time 1¼ hours

2 cloves garlic	1 teaspoon cinnamon powder
1 lb (500 g) apples	1 teaspoon chilli powder
8 oz (250 g) prunes	½ teaspoon freshly ground black
8 oz (250 g) dried apricots	pepper
1 cup cider vinegar	½ teaspoon ground cloves
1½ cups brown sugar	½ teaspoon ground coriander
1½ teaspoons salt	2 teaspoons powdered ginger

Preparation
Finely mince the garlic. Peel, core and dice the apples. Stone and chop the prunes. Chop the dried apricots. Mix all the fruit and garlic together and add the vinegar and sugar. Sprinkle with the salt and all the spices. Mix well.

Cooking

Bring gently to the boil over a low heat and continue to simmer for 1 hour, stirring frequently, until the chutney becomes soft and brown. Allow to cool, then bottle.

Thucahley foogaths
Stewed tomatoes

Serves 4 Cooking time 20 minutes

6 large tomatoes	2 tablespoons oil
2 cloves garlic	1 teaspoon salt
2 in (5 cm) fresh root ginger	1 teaspoon chilli powder
1 onion	1 tablespoon desiccated coconut

Preparation

Peel and chop the tomatoes. Finely mince the garlic and the ginger. Finely slice the onion.

Cooking

Heat the oil in a large heavy pan. Add the garlic, ginger and onion. Fry for 5 minutes, then add the tomatoes, salt and desiccated coconut. Continue to cook over a low heat for a further 15 minutes until the liquid has evaporated. Serve at once.

Boortha
Cucumber relish

Serves 6 Cooking time 10 minutes

3 small cucumbers	$\frac{1}{2}$ teaspoon chilli powder
1 onion	$\frac{1}{2}$ teaspoon salt
2 cloves garlic	2 tablespoons oil
1 green pepper	juice of 1 lemon
1 teaspoon powdered ginger	

Preparation

Peel and thickly slice the cucumbers. Finely chop the onion, garlic and green pepper.

Cooking
Boil the cucumber for 10 minutes, then drain thoroughly, add the chopped onion, garlic and pepper. Add the powdered ginger, chilli powder, salt, oil and lemon juice. Mix well and refrigerate for at least 2 hours before serving as a relish.

Bread
Chapatti

Serves 4 Cooking time 15 minutes

4 oz (125 g) wholewheat flour
½ cup water
plain flour for dusting

Preparation
Mix the flour and water to a firm dough. Dust a clean working surface with plain flour and put the dough on it. Knead until the dough becomes smooth. Roll the dough into a long sausage shape and cut with a sharp knife into pieces about the size of a golf ball. Roll out each ball until it is about 5-6 in (12.5-15 cm) in diameter.

Cooking
Heat a heavy pan over a medium heat. Do not add any oil or butter. Place one chapatti at a time on to the hot pan. When they puff, turn them over and cook the second side. Have a second element or gas ring on and place the puffed-up chappati directly in the flames or on the hot element so as to singe the high points. Only leave for a second or two – do not burn. Serve immediately.

Desserts
Orange and banana sorbet

Serves: 6

4 ripe bananas
1½ cups orange juice
3 cups yoghurt

1 tablespoon clear honey
mint leaves

Preparation

Chop the bananas and place in an electric blender. Add the orange juice, yoghurt and honey. Blend until smooth. Pour into a freezer tray and refrigerate until partly frozen. Return the mixture to the blender and blend again. Repeat the part-freezing process. When still mushy, blend once more. Finally, return to the freezer and this time leave it until it becomes firm. Serve in individual glasses or dishes and garnish with mint leaves.

Indian cheese cake

Serves 6 Cooking time 20 minutes

4 tablespoons blanched almonds	juice of 1 lemon
1 tablespoon butter	8 tablespoons sugar
10 cups milk	2 egg yolks

Preparation

Chop the almonds coarsely. Butter an ovenproof mould. Stud the bottom with the chopped almonds. Preheat your oven to 350°F, 190°C or Gas Mark 4.

Cooking

Bring the milk slowly to the boil, add the lemon juice, stir and remove from the heat. Allow the milk to curdle while cooling. Strain and place the curd in an electric blender. Add the sugar and egg yolks and blend until smooth. Pour the blended mixture into the mould on top of the almonds. Place the mould into your preheated oven and bake for 15 minutes or until set. Allow to cool, then chill thoroughly. Slide a sharp knife around the sides to loosen, before turning out of the mould and serving.

Banana hulva

Serves 6 Cooking time 25 minutes

6 large ripe bananas	$\frac{1}{2}$ teaspoon ground cardamom
2 tablespoons butter	$\frac{1}{2}$ teaspoon almond essence
1 cup water	pinch nutmeg
4 tablespoons sugar	2 tablespoons blanched slivered almonds

Preparation
Peel and slice the bananas.

Cooking
Fry the slice bananas in the butter for about 5 minutes. Remove from the heat and mash well. Add half the water and return to the heat. Stir continuously for 1 or 2 minutes. In a saucepan, bring the remaining water to the boil, add the sugar and stir until it has dissolved. Add the banana mixture to this second saucepan and boil gently together, stirring occasionally, for 12 minutes. By this time it should be nice and thick. Remove from the heat and whisk thoroughly until it becomes light and smooth. Add the ground cardamom, almond essence, nutmeg and almonds. Stir all together and pour into a serving bowl. Leave in a refrigerator for at least 4 hours before serving.

Meeta kayla
Banana puffs

Serves 6 Cooking time 10 minutes

2 cups self-raising flour	3 ripe bananas
4 oz (125 g) butter	4 tablespoons desiccated coconut
¼ cup milk	oil for deep-frying

Preparation
Sift the flour into a large bowl. Add the butter and the milk. Mix well, then knead. Roll out on a floured surface until it is about ¼ in (7 mm) thick. Cut out circles with a round 3 in (7.5 cm) biscuit cutter. Mash the bananas and add the coconut. Put a spoonful of the banana and coconut mixture on half of each pastry circle. Moisten the edges of the pastry with a little milk and fold one half over to form a half-circle with the banana mixture in the centre. Crimp the edges together. Make sure they are sealed. Make up all the pastry circles in this manner.

Cooking
Heat the oil in a deep saucepan. When very hot, carefully drop in the pastries. Deep-fry until golden brown. Drain thoroughly and serve either hot or cold.

Japan

As a visitor to Japan, studying the eating and cooking habits of the people, I observed two outstanding features of the country's cuisine that are unique.

Firstly, the lack of meat in the diet. Unlike Western countries and most of Asia, meat takes a secondary role in Japanese meals. When served in such dishes as *sukiyaki* and *shabu shabu*, it is wafer-thin and in very small quantities. The additional protein required is obtained by consumption of noodles and in particular *tofu*, a soy bean curd introduced by the Chinese.

Secondly, the artistry with which the food is prepared and presented. A Japanese meal needs a quiet room overlooking a tranquil garden with appropriate flower arrangements placed in the right position. The serving plates, bowls and platters, harmonise with the colours and textures of the season. And then, the food! Sculptured, carved and garnished with flowers and leaves. Small pink cherry blossoms fashioned out of *tofu* float in your bowl of *miso* in the spring. Green fans cut from cucumbers, and butterflies from lemon slices, grace a simple fish steak in summer. In Japan you eat with your eyes.

Unfortunately, the cultural heritage that created such skills is dying. No longer are the young women learning the art of Japanese cooking from their mothers. Western ideas and products have swamped the country to such an extent that traditional methods are in danger of dying out completely. On my last visit to Tokyo, however, I was fortunate and pleased to visit and receive instruction from Mr Toshio Yanagihara, the undisputed cooking master of Japan. Through his cooking school, TV programmes and books, he is keeping alive some of the traditional kitchen skills.

It was on the same visit to Tokyo that I ate the ultimate *sashimi*. I had eaten *sashimi* (raw fish) before on many occasions. To many it is unacceptable – but the same people will eat steak tartare and raw oysters.

I was the guest for lunch at a very expensive restaurant which seemed to be built in the centre of a bamboo grove. Tranquillity was the view through the window. Charming and ceremonial were the Geisha waitresses. The tatami mats we sat on were not so comfortable, but the food was magnificent. Individual trays were served with six perfectly sculptured hors d'oeuvres, each with its own delicate garnish. The soups served next were clear, with thin morsels of mushroom and fish floating in them. Rectangular plates with deliciously cooked marinated chicken breasts came next. Then, the *sashimi!* First, we were served the traditional selection of tiny fillets of salmon, tuna and prawns which melted in your mouth as well as chewy abalone and wafer-thin slices of puffer fish. Then came a small soup-like bowl with a lid on it. Expecting another soup, as it is traditional in Japan to have several soups throughout a meal, I lifted the lid. But to my surprise . . . no soup, but a live, swimming fish – not big, about one and a half inches long! My hosts informed me that this was 'very special *sashimi*' from north-western Japan and 'very, very good'. The thought of eating the fish didn't daunt me, but how was I going to get him in my mouth? Twenty minutes later, I learnt the method of catching a small fish with chopsticks, dipping it in the sauce and eating it. I would rather eat puffer fish and tuna any time!

From where and how such diets came from is lost in history. But as in other countries, the methods of cooking and the ingredients used have changed over the centuries. Great changes came about when Buddism was introduced from China and again when Japan opened her doors to the East. And now, Japan rapidly Westernises.

However, there are a few Japanese dishes which have been categorised by visitors as outstanding, and they are now cooked around the world in restaurants and homes. Two of these, most probably the two best known dishes from Japan, are included in this chapter: *sukiyaki* and *tempura*. *Sukiyaki* is a modern addition to the Japanese menu, being introduced only ninety years ago. *Tempura*, again, is a recent addition to the menu in terms of history, and was supposedly introduced by Spanish or Portuguese traders. As is the case with so many dishes, the origins are lost with time.

Soups
Suimona
Mixed vegetable soup

Serves 6 Cooking time 10 minutes

1 stick celery	6 cups chicken stock (see page 83)
3 mushrooms	½ teaspoon salt
4 slices canned bamboo shoots	1 teaspoon soy sauce
6 mange tout (snow peas)	

Preparation
Cut the celery, mushrooms, bamboo shoots and mange touts into matchstick pieces.

Cooking
Season the chicken stock with the salt and soy sauce. Place over a moderate heat and simmer. Place a saucepan of hot salted water

over a high heat and bring to the boil. Add the celery, mushrooms and sliced bamboo shoots and cook rapidly for 2 minutes. Add the mange tout and continue to cook for a further minute. Drain and rinse in cold water. Place a mixture of the cooked vegetables into each serving bowl and pour the hot soup over the vegetables. Serve immediately.

Chicken and mushroom soup

Serves 6 Cooking time 15 minutes

1 lb (500 g) chicken breast	2 tablespoons cornflour
2 teaspoons salt	½ lemon
2 tablespoons dry sherry	6 cups chicken stock (see page 83)
6 large mushrooms	2 teaspoons soy sauce

Preparation
Cut the chicken into small serving pieces, removing all skin. Sprinkle with the salt and sherry and leave to stand for 20 minutes. Clean the mushrooms. Remove the stems and slice each mushroom into about 6 thin slices. Drain the chicken pieces and retain the juices and sherry. Dust the chicken with the cornflour. Slice the lemon into 6 very thin slices.

Cooking
Bring a saucepan of water to the boil and add the chicken pieces. Poach them until they are cooked, about 10 minutes. Pour the chicken stock into a second saucepan, place over a moderate heat and bring to a simmer. Add the retained juices and sherry, the soy sauce and the sliced mushrooms to the stock and simmer for 5 minutes. Remove the mushrooms and place 6 slices in each soup bowl. To this, add some chicken pieces and then ladle on the boiling stock. Garnish with a thin slice of lemon and serve at once.

Onion and bean curd soup

Serves 6 Cooking time 5 minutes

1 can bean curd	6 cups chicken stock (see page 83)
3 spring onions	2 teaspoons soy sauce
peel of 1 lemon	1 teaspoon salt

Preparation
Drain the bean curd and cut into 12 small slices. Chop the spring onions, including the tops, into thin rings. Slice the lemon peel into long thin strips.

Cooking
Bring the chicken stock to the boil. Add the soy sauce and salt. Reduce to a simmer. Gently add the sliced bean curd and allow to heat through. Heat your 6 soup bowls and carefully place 2 pieces of bean curd in each. Sprinkle with the onion and place 2 thin slices of lemon peel in each bowl. Pour the boiling stock carefully into each bowl and serve at once.

Egg drop soup

Serves 6 Cooking time 8 minutes

24 mange tout	6 cups chicken stock (see page 83)
3 eggs	3 tablespoons soy sauce
salt	

Preparation
Top and tail the mange tout. Beat the eggs together thoroughly.

Cooking
Boil the mange tout in salted water until they are just cooked, about 3 minutes. At the same time, boil the chicken stock and add the soy sauce. Stir the stock slowly in a continuous circle and pour in the beaten eggs in one continuous thin stream. The eggs should cook in thread-like strips. Pour the soup into 6 bowls and garnish each bowl with 4 mange tout.

Pork and spinach soup

Serves 6 Cooking time 40 minutes

2 in (5 cm) fresh root ginger	1 teaspoon salt
1 lb (500 g) pork fillet	½ teaspoon pepper
1 tablespoon soy sauce	2 eggs
3 large leaves spinach	oil for frying
8 cups water	

Preparation

Grate the root ginger. Marinate the pork for 1 hour in the soy sauce. Turn the piece of pork over 2 or 3 times during this period. Wash and chop the spinach into pieces about 1 in (2.5 cm) square. Blend in an electric blender the grated ginger with a little water; strain and retain the liquid.

Cooking

Bring the water to the boil. Add the piece of pork and the marinade. Leave to boil until the pork is cooked, about 30 minutes. Remove the pork and retain the cooking liquid. Add the salt and pepper and the retained ginger juice to the cooking liquid. Slice the pork into very thin strips and return it to the stock. Place over a moderate heat. Add the spinach to the stock and cook for a further 1½ minutes, then remove from the heat. Heat the oil in a pan, beat the eggs and pour into the hot pan. Leave to cook. Pour out six bowls of soup. Turn the omelette over and let it just set. Remove and cut into very thin slices. Garnish each bowl with these thin strips and serve at once.

Seafood

Tempura
Prawns and vegetables in batter

Serves 6   Cooking time 20 minutes

2 carrots	1 egg
2 green peppers	6 tablespoons water
18 green beans	2 teaspoons salt
2 courgettes	4 tablespoons soy sauce
12 large cooked peeled prawns	4 tablespoons dry sherry
6 oz (185 g) plain flour	2 tablespoons horseradish sauce
	8 cups oil for deep-frying

Preparation
Peel and finely slice the carrots. Cut and remove the seeds and
stems from the peppers. Top and tail the beans and courgettes.
Cut all the vegetables into thin bite-size pieces and put to one
side. Wash the prawns under cold running water and pat dry. Sift
the flour into a bowl. Beat the egg and add to the flour together
with the water and salt. Blend thoroughly until you have a very
liquid batter. Mix together the soy sauce and the sherry and then
add the horseradish. This sauce may be served in individual
dipping bowls for each guest.

Cooking
Heat the oil until very hot. Dip all the vegetables and the prawns,
first into the batter, and then straight into the hot oil. Drain on
kitchen paper and serve immediately. Each piece of vegetable or
fish is dipped into the sauce before eating.

Salt-baked prawns

Serves 6   Cooking time 12 minutes

18 large green prawns	3 teaspoons powdered ginger
2 tablespoons dry sherry	3 tablespoons chicken stock (see page 83)
1 lb (500 g) sea salt	6 tablespoons soy sauce

Preparation
Peel the prawns, but leave intact the tails and heads. Devein and
wash under cold running water. Pat dry and place flat on a large

plate. Sprinkle with the sherry and leave for 1 hour. Insert skewers into each prawn, starting at the tail and ending up at the head. Put a layer of sea salt on a baking tray and then place the 18 skewered prawns on top. Cover completely with the rest of the salt. Preheat your oven to 425°F, 220°C or Gas Mark 7. Mix together thoroughly the ginger, chicken stock and soy sauce. Pour into 6 individual small dipping bowls.

Cooking
Place the baking tray into the hot oven and bake for 12 minutes. Wipe off the salt and serve. The prawns are dipped into the sauce before eating.

Lemon yaki
Fried lemon fish

Note: Lemon yaki is a classic Japanese dish which can show the artistry which goes into preparing a meal. The garnishes for these simply cooked fish steaks are beautiful fans fashioned from cucumbers and butterflies made from lemon slices.

Serves 6 Cooking time 8 minutes

2 lb (1 kg) salmon trout	2 lemons
2 teaspoons salt	1 cucumber
	3 tablespoons oil

Preparation
Cut the fish into 6 equal-sized steaks. Sprinkle with the salt and put to one side. Squeeze the juice from one of the lemons. Thinly slice the second lemon into 12 slices. Cut away with a sharp knife triangles, starting at the centre of the lemon slice and finishing at the rind, at opposite sides to each other. The remaining lemon forms the wings of the butterfly garnish. Cut the rind from the two triangles and these can form the feelers of each butterfly.

Cut the cucumber into 6 1½-in (3.75-cm) cubes. Cut each cube in thirds, so you end up with a thin slice of cucumber. Make parallel cuts up from one side almost to the other. Make about 7 to 8 such cuts. Now you can fan out the slice. Put the fans and butterflies on to each plate. Leaving enough room in the centre for the fish steak.

Cooking

Heat the oil in a very large heavy pan. Rinse off the salt from the steaks and pat dry. When the oil is just hot, put in the steaks and fry for about 4 minutes on each side. During the cooking of the first side, sprinkle with half the lemon juice. Turn the steaks over and sprinkle with the remaining lemon juice. When cooked, carefully lift out of the pan, place in the centre of each plate and serve.

Meat

Sukiyaki
Fried meat and noodles

Serves 6 Cooking time at table

Warishita sauce:
1 cup soy sauce
2 tablespoons sugar
3 tablespoons dry sherry
1 cup chicken stock (see page 83)

Sukiyaki:
2 lb (1 kg) steak, rump or sirloin

1 can bean curd
18 spring onions
3 onions
12 mushrooms
1 lb (500 g) watercress
6 eggs
8 oz (250 g) vermicelli noodles
2 oz (60 g) suet

Preparation

Mix all the sauce ingredients together thoroughly and pour into a jug. Have your butcher slice the steak into bacon-thin slices. Drain the bean curd. Slice the spring onions diagonally into 2-in (5-cm) slices. Slice the onions coarsely, about ½ in (1.25 cm) thick. Cut the mushrooms into quarters. Wash the watercress thoroughly and tear the leaves away from the stems. Arrange all the vegetables and meat on a large platter on your table. Break one egg into each serving bowl and place on the table.

Cooking

Boil the vermicelli noodles until they are just cooked. Drain and place on the table. Heat a large iron pan over a high heat and then bring it to the table and place over a table burner. Alternatively, plug in an electric frying pan and have on the table. Place the suet in the pan and with chopsticks grease the whole of the cooking pan. As the suet melts, toss in some of the meat and let it quickly brown. Turn it over once. Push to the side of the pan and toss in some vegetables and noodles. Pour in some of the sauce. Cook until the vegetables are just done; hot and still crisp. Serve the meat, noodles, vegetables and sauce in each bowl on top of the eggs and eat at once. Toss more meat into the pan and repeat.

Shabu-shabu
Japanese hot pot

Serves 4 Cooking time at table

Dipping sauce:
3 tablespoons sesame seeds
2 cups chicken stock
½ teaspoon chilli powder
1 tablespoon vinegar

Shabu-shabu:
2 lb (1 kg) steak, rump or sirloin
3 spring onions
6 mushrooms
1 can bamboo shoots
1 cabbage heart
1 can bean curd
8 cups chicken stock (see page 83)

Preparation
To make the dipping sauce, toast the sesame seeds in a heavy frying pan over a moderate heat until they start to pop. Transfer them into a grinder and grind to a fine powder. Add this to the chicken stock, soy sauce, chilli powder and vinegar. Stir well and put to one side.

Have your butcher slice the steak into bacon-thin slices. Diagonally slice the spring onions into 2-in (5-cm) lengths. Cut the mushrooms in half. Drain the bamboo shoots and slice finely. Cut the cabbage heart into bite-size pieces. Drain the bean curd. Arrange plates of mixed vegetables and meat, say, one plate for two people.

Cooking
Heat the chicken stock in a fondue pot over a moderate heat. When simmering, adjust seasoning and place on a table burner in the centre of your table. Arrange the plates of meat and vegetables around the fondue pot. Give each guest a small bowl of dipping sauce. Each guest, with chopsticks or a fondue fork, dips a piece of meat or vegetable into the simmering stock and cooks

it. It is then dipped into the sauce and eaten. You may wish to
supply additional dipping sauces: soy sauce, horseradish or chilli.
When all the meat and vegetables are eaten, the stock is then
served and eaten as soup.

Teppan yaki
Steak, prawns and vegetables

Serves 6 Cooking time 20 minutes

1½ lb (750 g) sirloin steak – 6
  steaks
1 teaspoon salt
1 teaspoon freshly ground pepper
2 teaspoons oil
6 large green prawns
1 tablespoon dry sherry
2 green peppers

6 spring onions
2 cloves garlic
3 tablespoons soy sauce
2 teaspoons sugar
1 tablespoon chicken stock (see
  page 83)
oil for frying

Preparation
Trim away any excess fat from the steaks. Sprinkle both sides
with the salt and half the pepper. Put to one side. Peel the
prawns, but leave the tail on, and devein. Wash under cold
running water and pat dry. Slice along the underside to make
butterflies. Open out flat and sprinkle with the sherry. Cut the
green peppers into quarters and remove the stem and seeds.
Coarsely chop 3 of the spring onions, including the green tops.
Finely chop the garlic and mince the remaining 3 spring onions.
Mix together 2 tablespoons of soy sauce, the sugar, chicken stock
and the minced spring onions. Pour into 6 small dipping bowls
and put to one side.

Cooking
Pour the oil into a large heavy pan and put over a high heat. Add
the steaks and fry quickly until they are cooked to the desired
degree. Remove and toss in the chopped garlic, the prawns, green
peppers and the chopped spring onions. Add the remaining soy
sauce and the remaining ½ teaspoon of pepper. Cook until the
prawns are just done, then remove. Serve the prawns, vegetables
and steaks together on warmed plates and give each guest a bowl
of dipping sauce.

Beef teriyaki
Beef steaks

Serves 6 Cooking time 12 minutes

2 lb (1 kg) rump steak	2 in (5 cm) fresh root ginger
5 tablespoons chicken stock (see page 83)	1 clove garlic
5 tablespoons soy sauce	1 tablespoon oil

Preparation
Trim the steak and cut into 6 equal portions. Mix together the chicken stock and the soy sauce. Coarsely chop the ginger and put into an electric blender with a little water. Blend until you have a pulp. Strain, then add 1 tablespoon of the liquid to your sauce. Finely chop the garlic and add to the sauce. Marinate the steaks in this mixture for 30 minutes.

Cooking
Heat a large heavy pan. Add the oil and then the steaks. Sauté quickly until they just start to brown. Pour over half the marinade and continue to cook for a further 5 minutes. Serve the steaks immediately.

Butaniku tsukeyaki
Pork steaks and vegetables

Serves 6 Cooking time 25 minutes

3 in (7.5 cm) fresh root ginger	6 spring onions
2 cloves garlic	2 carrots
3 tablespoons sesame seeds	2 leaves spinach
3 tablespoons soy sauce	1 tablespoon oil
1 tablespoon dry sherry	1 teaspoon salt
2 teaspoons sugar	½ teaspoon freshly ground pepper
6 lean pork steaks	

Preparation
Mince the ginger and garlic together. Toast the sesame seeds until just brown, then crush with a pestle in a mortar. Add the ginger and garlic together with the soy sauce, sherry and sugar. Mix together thoroughly. Place the pork steaks in a dish, pour

over the marinade and leave for 20 minutes. Cut the spring
onions, including the tops, diagonally, about 1 in (2.5 cm) wide.
Slice the carrots into thin strips. Coarsely chop the spinach.

Cooking

Heat the oil in a large heavy pan. Add the pork steaks and fry
quickly. Keep the marinade to one side. Season with the salt and
pepper. When the steaks are cooked, remove from the pan and
keep warm. Add the spring onions, carrots and the spinach to the
pan and cook for 5 minutes. Pour in the remaining marinade and
cook for a further minute. Serve the steaks and vegetables
together.

Niku dango
Pork and beef balls

Serves 6 Cooking time 45 minutes

8 oz (250 g) lean pork	3 cloves garlic
8 oz (250 g) lean beef	6 large mushrooms
1 teaspoon salt	2 in (5 cm) fresh root ginger
½ teaspoon freshly ground pepper	3 spring onions
2 tablespoons soy sauce	2 tablespoons oil
3 tablespoons cornflour	1 cup chicken stock (see page 83)

Preparation

Mince very finely the pork and beef. Add the salt, pepper and soy
sauce. Shape into walnut-size balls and dust thoroughly with the
cornflour. Crush and finely chop the garlic. Peel and slice the
mushrooms. Mince the ginger. Coarsely chop the spring onions.

Cooking

Heat the oil in a pan and brown the meatballs on all sides. Toss
in the garlic and mushrooms. Continue to cook for 3 minutes.
Add the chicken stock and minced ginger, cover the pan, reduce
the heat and simmer for 25 minutes. Toss in the spring onions
and cook for a further 5 minutes, then serve.

Poultry

Many Japanese recipes require *dashi,* a fish stock made from shaved, dried bonito fillets and seaweed. As both are somewhat difficult to obtain, I suggest the following recipe for chicken stock as a good substitute.

Chicken stock

Cooking time 1 hour 10 minutes

2 in (5 cm) fresh root ginger	2 teaspoons salt
3 spring onions	7 cups water
1 2-lb (1-kg) chicken	

Preparation
Chop the ginger coarsely. Chop the spring onions, including the green tops into 1-in (2.5-cm) pieces. Chop the chicken into pieces. Place all the ingredients in a large saucepan.

Cooking
Bring to the boil, reduce the heat and simmer for 1 hour. Skim the residue off the surface from time to time. Allow to cool. Skim off the fat and strain through butter muslin. You should have a nice clear chicken stock which can be stored for a few days in the refrigerator and used in many different Japanese dishes.

Grilled sesame chicken

Serves 6 Cooking time 12 minutes

2 tablespoons sesame seeds	1½ tablespoons vinegar
6 chicken breasts	1 tablespoon sugar
¾ cup dry sherry	1 lemon
3 tablespoons salad oil	6 spring onions
3 tablespoons soy sauce	

Preparation
Toast the sesame seeds in a dry pan until just brown and then grind them. Remove the chicken breasts from the bone and skin. Prepare a marinade by mixing the sherry, oil, soy sauce, vinegar,

sugar and the ground toasted sesame seeds. Leave the breasts to marinate for 30 minutes. Cut the lemon into 12 wedges. Clean and trim the spring onions.

Cooking

Preheat the grill to a high heat. Put the chicken in a baking dish and place under the grill. Baste several times with the marinade. Turn the breasts over after about 6 minutes and cook the other side. When golden brown and cooked right through, remove the chicken and slice diagonally into about 6 or 8 slices. Arrange each breast on individual plates in the original shape and garnish with the lemon wedges and spring onions. Serve immediately.

Chicken teriyaki
Marinated chicken

Serves 4 Cooking time 35 minutes

½ cup soy sauce	1 clove garlic
½ cup sweet sherry	2 in (5 cm) fresh root ginger
2 teaspoons sugar	1 4-lb (2-kg) chicken
½ teaspoon cayenne pepper	2 tablespoons oil

Preparation

Mix together the soy sauce, sherry, sugar and cayenne pepper. Chop the garlic very finely. Grate the ginger. Add the garlic and ginger to the sauce to make a marinade. Cut the chicken into serving pieces.

Cooking

Bring the marinade quickly to the boil in a small saucepan. Have the chicken ready in a large bowl. The moment the marinade boils, remove from the heat and pour over the chicken pieces. Leave to marinate for 30 minutes. Turn the chicken pieces over 3 or 4 times during this period. Drain the pieces of chicken. Heat the oil in a large heavy frying pan. Put in the chicken and fry until the chicken starts to brown. Reduce the heat and add 1 cup of the marinade and 1 cup of water. Cover the pan and simmer gently for about 20 minutes or until the chicken is tender. Drain the pieces of chicken and serve at once.

Yakitori
Grilled skewered chicken

Serves 6 Cooking time 12 minutes

1 small cucumber	3 tablespoons sugar
½ cup sweet sherry	1 3-lb (1.5-kg) chicken
½ cup soy sauce	3 teaspoons powdered ginger

Preparation
Grate the cucumber and put to one side. Mix together the sherry,
soy sauce and sugar. Stir until the sugar dissolves. Cut the
chicken into bite-size pieces and place on small metal or bamboo
skewers. Allow 3 or 4 per person. Place them flat in a large
shallow dish. Pour over the mixed marinade and leave for 5
minutes. Turn over once or twice.

Cooking
Preheat the grill to a moderate heat. Place the skewered chicken
under the grill and cook for 3 or 4 minutes on each side. Remove
from the grill. Brush with the remaining marinade and sprinkle
with the powdered ginger. Return to the grill and cook for a
further 1 or 2 minutes, or until the chicken is tender but not dried
out. Serve and garnish with the grated cucumber.

Toriniku no nanbanyaki
Grilled chicken

Serves 4 Cooking time 30 minutes

1 onion	2 tablespoons dry sherry
2 tablespoons horseradish sauce	2 tablespoons sugar
3 teaspoons powdered ginger	3 tablespoons soy sauce
	1 3-lb (1.5-kg) chicken

Preparation
Finely chop the onion and mix it with the horseradish sauce,
powdered ginger, sherry, sugar and soy sauce. Pour into a small
saucepan and place over a moderate heat. Bring to the boil,
reduce the heat and simmer for 5 minutes. Cut the chicken into
serving portions. Brush each portion thoroughly with the sauce
mixture and leave to stand for 20 minutes.

Cooking

Place the chicken under a hot grill and grill for 12 to 15 minutes on each side. Brush with the sauce several times during the cooking. Serve at once.

Kamo no tsukiyaki
Casseroled duck
Note: This needs to be marinated overnight.

Serves 4 Cooking time 2 hours

1 6-lb (3-kg) duck	½ teaspoon freshly ground pepper
1 in (2.5 cm) fresh root ginger	8 oz (250 g) mushrooms
½ cup soy sauce	2 onions
2 cups dry sherry	2 tablespoons oil
1 teaspoon salt	2 teaspoons cornflour

Preparation

Cut the duck into small serving portions and cut away as much fat as you can. Mince the ginger. Prepare a marinade by mixing together the soy sauce, sherry, salt, pepper and ginger. Marinate the duck portions in this overnight. Slice the mushrooms and onions.

Cooking

Heat the oil in a large flameproof casserole. Add the duck portions and brown. Add the sliced mushrooms and onions and fry for a further 5 minutes. Pour off all the fat and oil. Add the marinade, cover and allow to simmer for 1½ hours. Add a little water to the cornflour and add only if the liquid needs to be thickened. Serve

Vegetables and rice

Sunomora salad
Cucumber and prawn salad

Serves 6 Cooking time 5 minutes

½ cucumber	½ cup sugar
12 cooked peeled prawns	1 teaspoon salt
1 cup vinegar	

Preparation
Finely slice the cucumber. Make butterflies of the prawns by cutting three-quarters of the way through the body from the underside and folding open to form two butterfly wings.

Cooking
Heat the vinegar, sugar and salt in a saucepan until the sugar dissolves. Stir well, remove from the heat and refrigerate until required. Arrange the slices of cucumber on individual plates. Garnish with the butterfly prawns. Pour over the dressing and serve.

Glazed Japanese mushrooms and courgettes

Serves 6 Cooking time 6 minutes

3 courgettes	4 tablespoons soy sauce
10 oz (215 g) button mushrooms	1 tablespoon sugar
2 tablespoons salt	3 tablespoons toasted almond
3 tablespoons oil	slivers

Preparation
Slice the courgettes. Place them in a colander with the mushrooms and sprinkle with the salt. Leave them to stand for 30 minutes. Rinse under cold running water and pat dry with kitchen paper.

Cooking
Heat the oil in a large heavy pan over a moderate heat. When hot, toss in the mushrooms and the courgettes and cook for 3 minutes, stirring frequently. Add the soy sauce and sugar and continue to cook for a further 2 minutes, again stirring frequently.

Remove from the heat. With tongs, arrange the mushrooms and slices of courgettes on individual serving plates and sprinkle with the toasted almond slivers. Serve immediately

Marinated mushrooms

Serves 6 Cooking time 1 minute

36 small button mushrooms	3 tablespoons dry sherry
1 onion	2 tablespoons sugar
2 tablespoons soy sauce	1 teaspoon salt
4 tablespoons wine vinegar	

Preparation
Wash, dry, peel and remove the stems of the mushrooms. Mince the onion.

Cooking
Mix together the soy sauce, vinegar, sherry, sugar, salt and onion in a saucepan. Bring to the boil and boil for 1 minute. Pour straight over the mushrooms and leave in the refrigerator to marinate overnight. Drain and serve.

Sushi

Rice snacks

Notes: Someone once called *sushi* the 'Japanese sandwich'! But the only similarities to a Western sandwich is its 24-hour appeal. *Sushi* is an after-school snack; a canapé; a lunch; a dinner; a late night titbit; the bite at the station or while shopping. In Japan, it can be bought everywhere, costing from a modest few pence to unbelievable amounts, depending entirely on the ingredients.

Sushi is basically rice, to which vinegar is added – that is the bread in the sandwich. On top, inside, wrapped around – raw fish, cooked fish, pickles, vegetables and seaweed are placed.

Sushi rice

Serves 6-8 Cooking time 30 minutes

3 cups long-grain rice
3½ cups water

3 tablespoons vinegar
4½ tablespoons sugar
2 teaspoons salt

Preparation

Wash the rice and let it drain for 1 hour before cooking.

Cooking

Put the rice and the 3½ cups of water into a large heavy saucepan. Bring to the boil. Cover the saucepan, reduce the heat and simmer for 15 to 20 minutes. The rice is ready when it is still just slightly harder than you would normally cook rice. Remove from the heat and leave it to stand covered for 10 minutes. Put the vinegar, sugar and salt in a saucepan and bring to the boil. The moment it boils remove from the heat. Drain the rice and put into a large bowl. Pour over the vinegar evenly and fold gently, taking care not to break up the kernels. At the same time fan the rice. This helps to cool it and gives it a glossy lustre. Leave to cool.

Nigiri-zushi
Tokyo-style sushi

To assemble, shape about 2 tablespoons of the sushi rice into a finger, about 1 in by 2 in (2.5 cm by 5 cm). Put a little horseradish sauce on the rice. Then top with any of the following:

raw tuna, cut into small fillets;
prawns, parboiled and butterflied;
mackerel, cut into small fillets and marinated in lemon juice, sugar, vinegar and salt;
smoked salmon;
chicken breasts, cut into thin strips;
pickles;
omelette, cut into thin strips;
cucumber, cut into thin strips and salted;
mushrooms, marinated (see page 88);
spinach, chopped, parboiled and seasoned with salt, pepper and lemon juice;
oysters.

Indonesia

The Indonesian archipelago, washed by the South China Sea, Indian and Pacific Oceans, is an equatorial Eden and a gourmet's paradise. 'The Spice Islands' and 'The Morning of the World' are titles which indicate the exotic nature of the land, people and their culinary talents.

Stretching some 5000 kilometres, the patchwork of islands contains about 130 million inhabitants from a colourful background. Chinese, Hindus, Arabs and the Dutch all have, over the centuries, occupied, traded, and brought with them their own traditions, religions and eating habits.

To be known as 'The Spice Islands' is a folly, for in fact, Indonesia has only ever supplied nutmeg and mace from the islands of Ambon and Malacca and cloves from Ternate and Tidore. The extensive use of spices, which is so characteristic of the country's cooking, exists as a result of trading with Arabs and its Indian neighbour.

Predominantly Muslim, religion obviously plays a large part in the diet. However, pork, which is taboo to most Muslims, is eaten in large quantities on the island of Bali. A small Hindu fish in a large Muslim ocean. Contrary to most Hindu customs, beef is also eaten. On Bali, spit-roasted suckling pig is cooked and eaten on many festive occasions. Cut into small bite-size pieces, it is served on top of rice in a banana leaf cone and topped with a fiery hot *sambal* and called *babi guling*. It can be enjoyed in many Balinese restaurants and at most of the colourful religious rituals.

On a recent visit to Bali, which has been described by many romantics as 'Heaven' and 'Morning of the World', I was fortunate enough to be present at one such colourful ceremony. In a setting high on the hills beyond Denpassar, where terraced rice paddies and palm trees dominate the landscape, I came across a group of young women beautifully dressed in traditional garb, balancing metre-high pyramids of brightly coloured fruits, rice cakes and flowers on their heads. These *babanten* were being offered to the goddess *Batari Durga* after being blessed by the priest. In the courtyard of the temple, a bubbling festive air predominated. Vendors sold offerings of fruit and flowers and, of course, the *babi guling* was being roasted and served.

On the north-western island of Sumatra, one finds the most inventive cooks and the hottest chilli dishes. Thick, rich sauces containing numerous spices, fresh and dried herbs, nuts, coconut milk, chillies, onions and garlic are spread over seafood, poultry, fruit or buffalo. *Rendang*, named after the area in Sumatra where it is traditionally cooked, must be one of the most popular of the hot dishes. It is now found throughout Indonesia and gives rise to statements concerning the extremely hot chilli dishes, which many think are all the cooks of the archipelago have to offer.

Quite the contrary. On Java, the food is flavoured with not nearly as much chilli, but milder spices and a lot of palm sugar. Chilli *sambals,* mixed with onions, garlic, dried prawns, vinegar or coconut milk, are served as accompaniments as they are in all other areas.

For those who enjoy tropical fruit, Indonesia is a paradise, as the variety and quality are exciting. Rambutan, mangosteen, jackfruit, oranges, lemons, limes, melons, mangoes, salak, pineapple, guavas, lychees, fifteen varieties of bananas and the foul-smelling durian grow here. Much of the fruit is used in complex dishes. Bananas in particular are used in many and are also made into simple fritters and pancakes. The Indonesian cook does not prepare much in the way of desserts. Fresh fruit by itself is most traditional.

The basis for all meals is rice, plain, boiled or fried, Wherever you see the word *nasi* associated with a dish, it means it contains rice. *Nasi goreng* means fried rice; *nasi gurih,* coconut rice. However, this has not always been the case. In some areas the old custom of eating tapioca still prevails, even though it is ridiculously poor in protein.

The coconut palm, which, like paddy fields, are crowded on to every piece of fertile ground, supplies much to the economy and the kitchen. The fresh clear liquid from the centre of the coconut is consumed as a cooling, refreshing and highly nutritious drink. The flesh of the nut is grated and used as garnish, flavouring and texture in cooking. Pounded with water, the flesh renders the coconut milk which flavours and thickens many sauces and gravies. Even the palm fronds are woven into small baskets and mats on which food is served. As in many countries, Indonesia is dependent in so many ways on the coconut palm.

To a lesser extent, the banana is also important to the Indonesian cook. Apart from the uses I have described, a cook uses the large, flat, waxy leaves as a beautiful, disposable platter. Whole meals are served on large sections, the food beautifully presented and garnished with small flowers. From roadside stalls, food is sold in small packets, made from folded leaves, or as in the case with the Balinese, in cones *(babi guling)*.

Enjoy the cooking of Indonesia. Experiment with the textures and flavours and if palm fronds and banana leaves are available to you, try using them when serving, and garnish and present the food you cook with the care that cooks of Indonesia do. Once more, *Selamat mankan!*

Starters and snacks

Begedel djagung
Sweetcorn fritters

Serves 6 Cooking time 15 minutes

1 large can whole kernel sweetcorn	1 teaspoon chilli powder
1 egg	2 tablespoons self-raising flour
1 onion	1 tablespoon water
2 cloves garlic	6 oz (185 g) cooked peeled prawns
1 teaspoon salt	1 tablespoon oil
½ teaspoon pepper	

Preparation
Drain the sweetcorn and place in a bowl. Beat the egg and add to the sweetcorn. Finely chop the onion and the garlic. Add the chopped onion and garlic, the salt, pepper, chilli powder, flour and water to the sweetcorn. Mix well until you have a thick batter. Chop the prawns and fold into this mixture.

Cooking
Heat the oil in a small heavy pan and spoon the mixture in, 2 or 3 spoonfuls at a time. Allow to brown on one side before turning over and browning on the other side. Put in a warm oven until you have cooked all the mixture, then serve.

Rempeyek
Peanut crisps

Serves 6 Cooking time 15 minutes

6 oz (185 g) peanuts	1 teaspoon salt
1 onion	1 teaspoon ground coriander
1 clove garlic	½ teaspoon ground cumin
4 oz (125 g) rice flour	1 teaspoon chilli powder
3 tablespoons cornflour	oil for deep-frying
1 cup warm water	

Preparation
Remove the skins from the peanuts by roasting them in a moderate oven for 10 to 15 minutes and then rubbing them – the skins will fall off easily. Crush the peanuts slightly by rolling a

rolling pin over them 3 or 4 times. Finely chop the onion and garlic and mix with the crushed peanuts. Mix together the two flours and pour in the warm water. Beat until you have a lump-free batter. Season with the salt, coriander, cumin and chilli powder. Beat again thoroughly and leave to stand for 15 minutes. Add the peanuts, onions and garlic and stir.

Cooking
Heat the oil in a deep pan until it just reaches smoking point. Drop in the batter mixture, a tablespoon at a time, and fry until golden brown. Drain thoroughly and serve either hot or cold

Rempah
Coconut patties

Serves 4-6 Cooking time 15 minutes

8 oz (250 g) minced beef	1 egg
4 oz (125 g) desiccated coconut	1 teaspoon salt
1 clove garlic	½ teaspoon ground coriander
1 onion	¼ teaspoon ground cumin
	1 tablespoon oil

Preparation
Mix the minced beef and coconut together. Finely chop the garlic and onion. Beat the egg. Add the chopped garlic and onion, the egg, salt, coriander and cumin to the meat. Mix well and form into 6 or 8 small patties.

Cooking
Heat the oil in a small heavy pan and fry each patty on both sides until nicely brown. Place in a warm oven until they are all fried, then serve at once.

Soups
Soto ikan
Fish soup

Serves 6 Cooking time 40 minutes

1 lb (500 g) fish off-cuts – heads, bones, tails, etc.	2 onions
	1 carrot

2 potatoes
½ lemon
6 oz (185 g) white fish fillets
1 fresh red chilli
6 cups water
1 teaspoon turmeric

1 teaspoon chilli powder
2 cups coconut milk (see page 105)
4 oz (125 g) vermicelli noodles
½ teaspoon freshly ground pepper
1 teaspoon salt

Preparation

Chop the fish off-cuts. Finely chop the onions, carrot and potatoes. Peel the lemon and finely chop the peel. Squeeze the juice from the lemon. Cut the fish fillets into small bite-size pieces. Finely slice the red chilli.

Cooking

Bring the water to the boil. Add the fish off-cuts, the onions and carrots. Boil for 5 minutes. Add the lemon peel, lemon juice, turmeric and chilli powder and continue to boil for another 5 minutes. Add the potatoes. Reduce the heat and simmer for 20 minutes, then pass through a strainer. Remove all the fish off-cuts. Return the soup to the saucepan and add the coconut milk, vermicelli noodles and the fish fillets. Return to a moderate heat and simmer until the fish is cooked and the noodles are soft and translucent. Season with the pepper and salt. Garnish with the slices of red chilli and serve.

Sajoer

Prawn and vegetable soup

Serves 6 Cooking time 30 minutes

2 onions
2 cloves garlic
2 in (5 cm) fresh root ginger
2 teaspoons ground coriander
1 teaspoon ground cumin
2 teaspoons salt
1 teaspoon chilli powder
3 tablespoons oil

1 lb (500 g) green prawns
1½ lb (750 g) mixed vegetables –
   whatever is in season; choose 3 or
   4 that need the same cooking time
⅛ cabbage
peel of ½ lemon
8 cups coconut milk (see page 105)
1 bay leaf

Preparation

Coarsely chop the onions, garlic and ginger. Put all three into an electric blender, add the coriander, cumin, salt, chilli powder and a little of the oil. Blend into a smooth paste. Peel and devein the prawns. Wash under cold running water and pat dry. Chop all the vegetables. Shred the cabbage. Grate the lemon peel.

Cooking

Heat the oil in a large saucepan. Add the blended ingredients and fry for 3 minutes, stirring continuously. Add the coconut milk and bring to the boil. Add the mixed vegetables and the cabbage together with the bay leaf and the grated lemon peel. Continue to cook gently for 20 minutes, then add the prawns. Cook for a further 5 minutes, then serve.

Soto danging
Beef soup

Serves 6 Cooking time 40 minutes

2 lb (1 kg) shin beef	2 in (5 cm) fresh root ginger
10 cups water	1 teaspoon turmeric
6 oz (185 g) green prawns	2 teaspoons salt
2 onions	6 spring onions
3 cloves garlic	

Preparation

Cover the meat with the water and bring to the boil. Reduce the heat and simmer for 20 minutes. Remove the meat and slice finely. Return it to the liquid and leave to cool on one side. In the meantime, peel and devein the prawns. Wash under cold running water and pat dry. Put them into an electric blender with a little water and blend into a smooth paste. Remove and strain thoroughly. Retain the liquid and discard the prawn pulp. Add the prawn liquid to the pan containing the meat. Mince the onions, garlic and ginger and add to the pan together with the turmeric and salt. Coarsely chop the spring onions and put to one side.

Cooking

Place the pan containing the stock and meat over a medium heat and gently bring back to a simmer. Continue to simmer until the meat is tender. Garnish with the chopped spring onions and serve.

Seafood

Sambal goreng pedas
Prawn sambal

Serves 4 Cooking time 10 minutes

3 fresh red chillies	1 lb (500 g) green prawns
1 onion	1½ cups coconut milk (see page 105)
2 cloves garlic	2 tablespoons lemon juice
4 tomatoes	2 tablespoons sugar
2 tablespoons oil	1 teaspoon salt

Preparation
Finely chop the red chillies, onion and garlic. Mix all together.
Cut the tomatoes into quarters and put to one side. Peel and
devein the prawns. Wash under cold running water and pat dry.

Cooking
Heat the oil in a large heavy pan. When hot, toss in the chopped
chillies, onion and garlic, and fry for 3 minutes. Add the prawns
and continue to fry for a further minute. Pour in the coconut milk
and lemon juice. Add the sugar and salt. Stir well and simmer
until the prawns are tender. Serve immediately.

Iekan bandang panggang
Baked fish

Serves 6 Cooking time 25 minutes

4 lb (2 kg) mackerel	1 onion
2 cloves garlic	2 tablespoons butter
2 teaspoons salt	1 tablespoon soy sauce
1 teaspoon freshly ground black	juice of 1 lemon
pepper	1 teaspoon chilli powder

Preparation
Have your fishmonger split and bone the fish. Cut the onion into
quarters. Put into an electric blender the garlic, salt, freshly
ground black pepper and the quartered onion. Blend into a paste
and rub into the fish. Soften the butter and use a little to grease a
baking dish. Put in the fish. Blend together the remaining butter,

soy sauce, lemon juice and chilli powder. Pour this mixture over the fish. Preheat the oven to 375°F, 190°C or Gas Mark 5.

Cooking

Place the baking dish in the preheated oven and bake the fish for 25 minutes. Baste several times during the cooking and turn the fish over at least once.

Sambal oedang
Spiced prawns

Serves 6 Cooking time 16 minutes

2 onions	3 teaspoons raw sugar
3 cloves garlic	2 in (5 cm) fresh root ginger
1 teaspoon salt	1 lb (500 g) green prawns
1 teaspoon chilli powder	3 teaspoons oil
juice of ½ lemon	1½ cups coconut milk (see page
peel of ½ lemon	105)

Preparation

Chop the onions coarsely and blend in an electric blender with the garlic, salt, chilli powder, lemon juice, lemon peel, sugar and ginger. Peel and devein the prawns. Wash under cold running water and pat dry.

Cooking

Heat the oil in a heavy pan and add the blended ingredients. Fry for 3 minutes, stirring continuously. Add the prawns, reduce the heat and continue to stir-fry for a further 3 minutes. Add the coconut milk and simmer for 10 minutes. Cool and chill before serving.

Meat
Kambling rendang
Lamb rendang

Serves 4 Cooking time 30 minutes

1½ lb (750 g) boned lamb	2 tablespoons chilli powder
1 onion	½ teaspoon turmeric
peel of ½ lemon	2 teaspoons salt
1 cup desiccated coconut	2 cups coconut milk (see page 105)
8 tablespoons oil	1 teaspoon sugar

Preparation

Cut the lamb into thin slices, then into 2-in (5-cm) squares. Mince the onion and lemon peel. Spread the coconut over the surface of a large heavy pan and place over a high heat. Stir continuously, and when the coconut becomes golden brown, remove from the heat and pound into a fine powder.

Cooking

Heat the oil in a large heavy pan. When the oil is hot, toss in the minced onion and lemon peel, stir well and add the chilli powder, turmeric and salt. Stir-fry for 1 minute, then add the lamb and continue to fry until the meat is well coated with the spices and is browned. Pour in the coconut milk and add the sugar and powdered coconut. Continue to simmer gently, uncovered, until the liquid has evaporated, then serve at once.

Babi guling
Roast suckling pig

Serves 10-12 Cooking time 2½ hours

1 10-12 lb (5-6 kg) suckling pig	3 teaspoons turmeric
2 in (5 cm) fresh root ginger	1 teaspoon grated nutmeg
peel of ½ lemon	1 teaspoon freshly ground black
6 cloves	pepper
4 tablespoons oil	3 onions
3 teaspoons chilli powder	4 cloves garlic

Preparation

Have your butcher prepare the piglet. Wash it and wipe dry.
Blend the root ginger in an electric blender with the lemon peel,
cloves and a little of the oil. When blended, add the chilli powder,
turmeric, grated nutmeg and freshly ground black pepper. Finely
chop the onions. Crush and chop the garlic. Preheat the oven to
375°F, 190°C or Gas Mark 5.

Cooking

Heat the remaining oil in a pan and toss in the chopped onions
and garlic. Fry for 4 or 5 minutes, then add the blended spices
and continue to fry for a further 5 minutes. Place all the fried
ingredients into the prepared piglet and sew up the opening. Rub
the surface with the salt and secure the piglet on to a rotisserie.
Place in the preheated oven and put a baking tray under the
piglet to collect the juices. Spit roast for 2½ hours. Baste several
times during cooking with the liquid that collects in the baking
tray. Slice and serve.

Pepper steak

Serves 4 Cooking time 25 minutes

2 lb (1 kg) rump steak	5 tablespoons soy sauce
3 onions	3 medium-sized tomatoes
4 cloves garlic	2 tablespoons butter
3 teaspoons freshly ground black pepper	1 teaspoon oil
2 tablespoons sugar	2 teaspoons ground cinnamon

Preparation

Cut the steak into bite-size pieces, then beat them flat with a meat
mallet or rolling pin. Coarsely chop 1 of the onions. Cut the garlic
cloves in half. Put the onions and garlic into an electric blender
and add the freshly ground black pepper, sugar and soy sauce.
Blend until you have a smooth paste. Coat all the meat with the
paste and leave to marinate for 1 hour. In the meantime, finely
slice the remaining onions. Peel and chop the tomatoes.

Cooking

In a large pan, melt the butter and just as it starts to froth, add
the oil. Toss in the sliced onions and fry until just transparent.

Add the meat and all the marinade. Fry until the meat starts to brown, stirring occasionally. Add the cinnamon and the tomatoes. Continue to fry for 1 minute, then pour in enough boiling water to just cover the meat. Reduce the heat and leave to simmer, uncovered, until most of the liquid has evaporated and the meat is tender. Serve at once.

Hot Java meatballs

Serves 6 Cooking time 10 minutes

1 lb (500 g) minced beef steak	1 tablespoon ground coriander
2 onions	1 teaspoon ground cumin
3 cloves garlic	1 tablespoon soy sauce
1½ teaspoons chilli powder	1 tablespoon demerara sugar
2 eggs	juice of ½ lemon
1 teaspoon anchovy sauce	8 cups oil

Preparation

Place the minced beef steak in a large bowl. Finely chop the onions and the garlic and add to the meat. Sprinkle with the chilli powder. Lightly beat the eggs and add to the meat together with the anchovy sauce, coriander, cumin, soy sauce, sugar and lemon juice. Mix thoroughly, then form golf ball-sized meatballs with your hands.

Cooking

Heat the oil in a deep saucepan until just smoking, then deep-fry until golden brown. Drain thoroughly on kitchen towel and serve either hot or cold.

Rendang
Beef rendang

Serves 6 Cooking time 40 minutes

1½ lb (750 g) rump steak	½ teaspoon turmeric
2 in (5 cm) fresh root ginger	7 teaspoons chilli powder
1 onion	peel of ½ lemon
1 teaspoon coriander seeds	coconut milk (see page 105)
2 cloves garlic	salt

Preparation

Cut the steak into bite-size pieces. Chop the ginger and onion. In an electric blender, blend the coriander seeds, ginger, onion, garlic, turmeric and chilli powder with a little of the coconut milk. Finely grate the lemon peel.

Cooking

Pour the blended spices into a large heavy pan, add the coconut milk, and the grated lemon peel. Toss in the meat and bring to the boil. Add the salt. Continue to boil until the sauce is almost dry, then reduce the heat to low. Continue to cook until the oil from the coconut starts to appear. Now continue to fry the meat and spices in the oil, stirring all the time, until the sauce is really dry and the meat is dark brown. This stage of cooking must be done with the utmost care. Do not let it burn. Serve at once.

Babi kecap
Sweet pork

Serves 4 Cooking time 25 minutes

1½ lb (750 g) lean pork	4 tablespoons oil
2 teaspoons salt	1 cup chicken stock
1 teaspoon pepper	3 teaspoons tomato paste
¼ cup flour	3 tablespoons brown sugar
2 onions	2 tablespoons soy sauce
3 cloves garlic	4 sprigs parsley

Preparation

Slice the pork very thinly. Sprinkle with the salt, pepper and flour. Put to one side. Finely chop the onions and garlic.

Cooking

Heat the oil in a large heavy pan. Add the seasoned and floured pork. Fry until golden brown, remove, drain and put to one side. Toss the onion and garlic into the pan with the remaining oil and fry until the onions are just transparent. Add the chicken stock, tomato paste and brown sugar. Stir well and cook for 1 or 2 minutes, reduce the heat and add the pork slices. Add the soy sauce and continue to cook for 10 minutes. Increase the heat and finish the cooking after 5 minutes, by which time all the liquid should be absorbed. Garnish with the parsley and serve.

Dendeng ragi
Crispy fried meat

Serves 4 Cooking time 1 hour

1½ lb (750 g) rump steak
5 dried red chillies
3 teaspoons coriander seeds
2 teaspoons cumin seeds
8 black peppercorns

2 onions
4 cloves garlic
2 cups desiccated coconut
juice of 1 lemon
5 tablespoons oil

Preparation
Cut your rump steak into wafer-thin slices with a very sharp knife. Cut each slice into small pieces about 2 in (5 cm) square. Grind in an electric blender the red chillies, coriander seeds, cumin seeds and the black peppercorns. Chop the onion and garlic and add to the blender with a little water. Blend until you have a smooth paste. Moisten the desiccated coconut with a little water.

Cooking
Pour the blended paste into a saucepan, add the meat and the desiccated coconut. Cover and gently stew without the addition of any other liquid until the meat is cooked. Remove the lid, add the lemon juice and 3 tablespoons of water. Continue to cook until it is quite dry. Heat the oil in a large pan and add the meat and dried-out paste. Continue to fry, stirring occasionally, until the meat is crisp. This will take about 30 minutes.

Poultry
Ajam panggang (1)
Grilled chicken breasts

Serves 4 Cooking time 1 hour

2 medium onions
1 in (2.5 cm) fresh root ginger
3 cloves garlic
2 fresh green chillies

2 cups coconut milk (see page 105)
1 teaspoon turmeric
2 teaspoons salt
4 chicken breasts

Preparation

Chop the onions, ginger, garlic and green chillies and place in an electric blender. Add ½ cup coconut milk and the turmeric. Blend thoroughly until you have a thick paste, then add the rest of the coconut milk and the salt. Cut each chicken breast into 4 pieces.

Cooking

Pour the blended ingredients into a heavy pan and bring to the boil. Add the chicken pieces and simmer until all the liquid has evaporated. Remove the chicken pieces, place under a hot grill and cook for 5 to 6 minutes on each side until they are golden brown. Serve at once. You may serve the cooking sauce as well.

Pejjec ajam
Coconut chicken

Serves 4 Cooking time 25 minutes

1 lb (500 g) cold roast chicken meat	2 tablespoons oil
2 onions	1 teaspoon ground coriander
3 cloves garlic	½ teaspoon chilli powder
2 in (5 cm) fresh root ginger	3 cups coconut milk (see page 105)

Preparation

Cut the chicken into small bite-size pieces. Finely slice the onions. Crush and chop the garlic. Grate the ginger.

Cooking

Heat the oil in a large heavy pan. Toss in the onions, garlic and ginger. Fry for about 5 minutes, then add the ground coriander, chilli powder and the coconut milk. Simmer gently for 1 minute, then add the chicken and continue to cook, uncovered, for 15 minutes, stirring occasionally. Serve.

Ajam panggang (2)
Grilled chicken

Serves 4 Cooking time 45 minutes

1 4-lb (2-kg) chicken	3 cloves garlic
2 onions	3 tablespoons chilli powder

2 teaspoons prawn paste   2 teaspoons sugar
2 teaspoons oil   1 teaspoon salt
peel of ½ lemon   juice of ½ lemon
1 cup coconut milk (see page 105)

Preparation
Cut the chicken through the breast, but keep the back intact.
Open it out flat and skewer the legs and wings down flat. Chop
the onions and garlic. Blend in an electric blender the chilli
powder, onions, garlic, prawn paste and oil. Coat the entire
surface of the chicken with this mixture. Grate the lemon peel.
Mix together the coconut milk, grated lemon peel, sugar, salt and
lemon juice and pour into a pan large enough to hold the flat
chicken. Put in the chicken.

Cooking
Place the pan over a medium heat and bring gently to the boil.
Ladle the liquid over the chicken from time to time and leave to
simmer until the chicken is tender and the cooking liquid is dried
out. Remove the chicken and place under a hot grill. Spoon over
the remaining sauce from the pan during grilling. Serve as soon
as the chicken is golden brown.

Coconut milk, rice and vegetables
Coconut milk

3 cups desiccated coconut
4 cups hot water

Preparation
Blend the desiccated coconut and the hot water together in an
electric blender or leave the coconut to steep in the hot water for
20 minutes. Either way, pass through a strainer and retain the
white coconut milk.

Nasi goreng
Fried rice

Serves 4 Cooking time 12 minutes

3 eggs	3 celery stalks
1 lb (500 g) cold cooked chicken meat	2 tablespoons oil
1 onion	8 oz (250 g) cooked peeled prawns
2 fresh green chillies	3 cups cold cooked long grain rice
2 cloves garlic	2 tablespoons soy sauce

Preparation

Lightly beat the eggs. Cut the chicken into very thin strips. Finely chop the onion and green chillies. Crush and chop the garlic. Finely chop the celery.

Cooking

Heat half the oil in a pan. When hot, pour in the beaten eggs and cook until set. Remove from the pan, leave to cool, then cut into thin strips. In a second large pan, heat the remaining oil. When hot, toss in the onions, chillies and garlic. Fry for 5 minutes stirring 2 or 3 times. Add the chicken, prawns and celery. Stir and continue to cook for 3 minutes. Add the cooked rice, pour in the soy sauce, stir once or twice and leave for about 3 minutes. Remove from the pan and place in a preheated serving dish. Garnish with the strips of egg and serve at once.

Nasi gurih
Coconut rice

Serves 6 Cooking time 40 minutes

1 lb (500 g) long-grain rice	3½ cups coconut milk (see page 105)
peel of ½ lemon	½ teaspoon salt

Preparation

Wash the rice under cold running water until the water runs clear. Grate the lemon peel very finely.

Cooking

Put the coconut milk, grated lemon peel and salt into a saucepan and bring to the boil. Add the rice and cover the pan loosely. Boil for about 10 minutes, or until steam starts to escape through holes in the surface of the rice. Place an abestos mat under the saucepan and fit the lid tightly. Reduce the heat to low and leave for a further 10 minutes or if you are using electricity, turn on a second electric plate to as low as possible. Place the saucepan and asbestos mat on this plate and leave for a further 20 minutes.

Gado gado
Cooked vegetable salad

Serves 6   Cooking time 40 minutes

3 spring onions	2 carrots
1 can bean sprouts or 2 cups fresh	3 eggs
1 small cucumber	2 tablespoons oil
2 stalks celery	4 fresh red chillies
8 oz (250 g) French beans	3 cloves garlic
½ small cabbage heart	8 oz (250 g) jar crunchy peanut butter
3 potatoes	4 cups coconut milk (see page 105)
	2 teaspoons lemon juice

Preparation
Chop the spring onions. Drain the bean sprouts. Chop the cucumber coarsely. Finely chop the celery. Diagonally cut the French beans. Shred the cabbage. Peel and cut the potatoes in half. Peel and cut the carrots into thin strips.

Cooking
Lightly boil the French beans for 2 or 3 minutes, then drain and put to one side. Blanch the cabbage. Boil the potatoes until cooked, then slice. Parboil the carrots. Hardboil the eggs, then peel and cut into quarters. Heat the oil in a small pan and fry the red chillies for 3 or 4 minutes, then remove and drain. Fry the garlic in the same way. Blend in an electric blender the garlic and chillies, then add the peanut butter, coconut milk and sugar and blend all together. Pour into a small saucepan and add the lemon juice. Bring to the boil and allow the sauce to thicken but still retain its pouring consistency.

Mix together the bean sprouts, cucumber, French beans, cabbage, potatoes and carrots in a large serving bowl. Pour over the cooled peanut sauce and garnish with celery, spring onions and eggs.

Desserts

Serigaja

Coconut pudding

Serves 6 Cooking time 45 minutes

3 tablespoons butter	$\frac{1}{2}$ teaspoon cinnamon powder
1 cup sugar	6 eggs
5 tablespoons flour	2 cups coconut milk (see page 105)

Preparation

Cream the butter and sugar together. Add the flour and cinnamon and mix well. Separate the eggs and put the egg whites to one side. Add the egg yokes one at a time to the flour and cinnamon and beat continuously until the mixture is light and fluffy. Gently pour in the coconut milk and beat again. Beat the egg whites until very stiff, then fold into your mixture. Pour into a large buttered ovenproof bowl or 6 individual custard cups and place in a baking tray. Pour enough hot water into the try to come three-quarters of the way up the bowl or cups. Preheat the oven to 375°F, 190°C or Gas Mark 5.

Cooking

Put the baking tray with the bowl or cups into the preheated oven and bake for 45 minutes. Cook, then chill in the refrigerator before turning out and serving.

Malaysia and Singapore

Rather than trying to divide the subtleties that exist between Malaysia and the island city of Singapore, I have opted to put them together in one chapter. After all, the people are the same – a harmonious mixture of the descendants of Indian traders, immigrant Chinese and indigenous Malays. All have their own styles of cooking and have maintained the flavours and textures over generations, only borrowing ingredients from other cultures after decades of sampling.

In many cases a Chinese dish cooked in its original form in mainland China will taste bland compared with the same dish now prepared in Kuala Lumpur or Singapore. The addition of the much used local chilli opens up a whole new aspect to traditional Chinese cuisine. This style of Malaysian Chinese cooking is very evident to all travellers to Malaysia and, in particular, Singapore. As soon as dusk falls the ingenious Chinese penetrate every corner of the towns and cities with their compact mobile kitchens. As each 'hawker' specialises in one dish, one can feast all night on delicious food that is cooked in a matter of seconds before your eyes.

At the same venues the symbol of Malaysian food, *satay,* is sure to be sold as well. *Satay* are bamboo skewers of meat smothered in a rich chilli and peanut sauce and served with cucumber. The recipe was adopted centuries ago from the Arabic kebab, and now is a classic dish in its own right. The Arabs influenced the Malays greatly by introducing them to the delights of spices which they purchased from the visiting Indian traders.

Most Malays are Muslims and their diets are controlled by strict taboos. However, Malaysia is a large importer of pork, the ultimate taboo. It is not for the Malaysian cooking pots however. The Chinese, whose basic cooking skills revolve around pork, have overcome the prejudice of their neighbours and prepare the meat side by side with non-pork-eating Malays.

Many of the dishes that are found in Malaysia can also be found in Indonesia. Easy to understand, when you realise that the whole archipelago was at one time one country known as 'The Kingdom of Srivijaja'. *Rendangs, gulehs, ajars, sambals, sambal gereng, clondang* and *opor* are all dishes that appear on the menus of both countries. For the sake of simplicity, I have not tried to associate any one dish with either one country or the other, but have listed the recipes in the chapters as I came across them in my research.

While in Singapore I was fortunate enough to meet Mrs Lee Chin Koon, mother of Lee Kuan Yew, Prime Minister of

Singapore. Mrs Lee is an authority on Nonya cooking and has written the only complete book on the subject. This is the cooking of the Straits-born Chinese – a style which, unlike all other cooking in Malaysia, is a complete amalgam of two cultures. Mrs Lee explained in great detail the history of her people before taking me around the city to discover, not only Nonya food being sold from hawker stalls and restaurants, but also many of the great traditional cooks from mainland China who have made Singapore their home.

Nonya cooking is sometimes known as *Lauk embok embok*. The Chinese immigrants, who, generations ago, went to Malacca and Penang as labourers for the British, married local Malay women. The women who controlled the cooking pots obviously used the ingredients and cooking styles of Malaysia. However, their non-Muslim Chinese husbands influenced them to the extent of using pork as well as other Chinese ingredients. The result is a complicated cooking style that takes years to learn and is very difficult to adapt, which is a pity, but it is most probably one of the reasons why this unique style of cooking seems to be dying out. Hence, I have only included very few of these dishes in this book. As Mrs Lee Chin Koon explained to me, you need all the ingredients found in a Malaysian, Indonesian and a Chinese kitchen as well as the patience to learn one of the most fastidious styles of cooking by trial and error!

Malaysian cooking is in comparison extremely simple. Lots of fresh vegetables and chicken which most Malaysians grow and rear. An abundance of tropical fruits is eaten fresh and cooked. Rambutan, durian, mangosteen, breadfruit, pineapples, bananas, lemons and limes, to name just a few, are harvested and sold daily.

The most important of all ingredients in Malaysian cooking must be fish. In fact a 'prawn paste', known as *blachan*, is the base flavour of many dishes. The prawns are caught in the South China Sea and the Malaccan Straits in such large quantities that not only is there enough for their paste, but also for eating fresh, dried or in powdered form. The rest is exported.

All the food in Malaysia is served in a simple fashion on a single plate or, in many cases, on a banana leaf. A spoon, fork, or just fingers, are used. There is no need to overcomplicate the

presentation as the flavours and textures have enough to tell on
their own.

Starters and snacks

Murtabar
Meat pancakes

Serves 6 Cooking time 25 minutes

1½ lb (750 g) wholewheat flour	12 oz (375 g) minced beef
2 eggs	1 teaspoon salt
1 fresh red chilli	3 oz (90 g) butter
1 tomato	3 tablespoons oil
1 onion	

Preparation
Put the flour into a large bowl, add water gradually and mix until
you have a stiff dough. Cover the bowl with a dampened teatowel
and put to one side for 30 minutes. Beat the eggs until frothy and
put to one side. Finely chop the red chilli, tomato and onion and
mix together with the minced beef. Add the salt and mix well.
After the dough has been left for 30 minutes, remove from the
bowl and knead on a floured surface until smooth. Divide into 6
equal balls and in turn roll out each one as thinly as possible.

Cooking
Heat half the butter in a heavy pan and fry each pancake for just
a few moments on each side. Do not leave to brown. In a second
large heavy pan heat 2 tablespoons of the oil and fry the meat and
vegetable mixture, until the meat is cooked and the onion has
become transparent. Spread the beaten eggs on to one side of
each of the six pancakes. Divide the cooked meat into 6 equal
portions and place in the centre of each pancake. Fold the
pancakes over, then seal the edges by pressing firmly together.
Add the rest of the butter and the remaining tablespoon of oil to
the original pan and place over a moderate heat. Fry each of the
pancakes until golden brown, drain and serve.

Soups

Sookmuytont
Creamed corn soup

Serves 6 Cooking time 10 minutes

breast meat of 1 chicken
½ tablespoon salt
½ tablespoon sherry
½ teaspoon pepper

3 cups chicken stock (see page 83)
4 tablespoons cornflour
1-lb (500-g) can creamed corn

Preparation

Remove the flesh from the chicken breasts and mince finely. Add the salt, sherry, pepper, 3 tablespoons of the chicken stock and the cornflour. Mix well.

Cooking

In a medium-sized saucepan, heat the remaining chicken stock and the creamed corn. When it is boiling, add the chicken mixture and immediately turn off the heat. Stir for 1 or 2 minutes and serve immediately.

Malaysian chicken soup

Serves 6 Cooking time 1½ hours

1 4-lb (2-kg) chicken
2 onions
8 cups water
1 tablespoon salt

3 tablespoons oil
1½ cups long-grain rice
½ teaspoon freshly ground pepper

Preparation

Disjoint the chicken. Slice one of the onions. Quarter the second onion and put to one side.

Cooking

Boil the water in a large saucepan. Add the salt, the chicken pieces and the quartered onion and boil for 1 hour until the chicken is tender. Strain the cooking liquid and put to one side. Remove the bones and skin from the chicken and dice the flesh. In a large heavy pan, heat 2 tablespoons of the oil. Toss in the sliced onion and fry gently until just turning brown. Remove the onions from the pan and put to one side. Add the remaining oil to the pan and toss in the rice. Stir frequently until the rice starts to brown. While the rice browns, bring the strained stock to the boil, then add the browned rice. Sprinkle with the pepper and continue to simmer for 15 minutes or until the rice is cooked. Add the diced chicken, stir and let it heat through. Serve with the browned onions sprinkled on top.

Boeboe ayam
Chicken and rice soup

Serves 6 Cooking time 1½ hours

2 large onions	3 tablespoons oil
1 3-lb (1.5-kg) chicken	1½ cups long-grain rice
2 teaspoons salt	1 teaspoon freshly ground pepper
8 cups water	½ teaspoon chilli powder

Preparation
Finely slice the onions.

Cooking
Put half the sliced onions into a saucepan with the chicken, salt and 8 cups of water. Place over a moderate heat and bring to the boil. Reduce the heat and simmer for 1 hour. Strain and retain the stock. Remove the skin from the chicken and cut away all the flesh. Dice and put to one side. Heat 2 tablespoons of the oil in a small pan and brown the remaining sliced onions. Remove and put to one side. Heat the remaining tablespoon of oil in the pan and brown the rice, stirring continuously. Bring the stock to the boil and add the rice, pepper and chilli powder. Reduce the heat and simmer for 20 minutes or until the rice is cooked. Add the diced chicken and continue to simmer for 2 minutes. Serve garnished with the browned onions.

Seafood
Singapore chilli crab

Serves 4 Cooking time 20 minutes

3 uncooked crabs	2 teaspoons sugar
1 egg	1 teaspoon salt
3 cloves garlic	1 tablespoon oil
4 fresh red chillies	1 cup chicken stock
1 in (2.5 cm) fresh root ginger	2 teaspoons cornflour
4 tablespoons tomato sauce	1 tablespoon vinegar

Preparation
Thoroughly clean the crabs and discard the inedible bits. Cut the crabmeat into small pieces. Crack the claws. Beat the egg and put to one side. Finely chop the garlic. Blend together the chillies, ginger, tomato sauce, sugar and salt in an electric blender.

Cooking
Heat the oil in a large pan and toss in the chopped garlic and crab. Cook for 2 minutes, then pour in the chicken stock, cover and leave to simmer for 15 minutes. Add the blended ingredients together with the cornflour, vinegar and beaten egg. Stir continuously until the sauce thickens, then serve.

Fish moolie

Serves 4 Cooking time 20 minutes

1 in (2.5 cm) fresh root ginger	1 lb (500 g) fish (snapper, bream)
12 spring onions	2 tomatoes
1 teaspoon turmeric	5 tablespoons oil
1 teaspoon ground coriander	coconut milk (see page 105)
¼ teaspoon ground cumin	½ tablespoon sugar
½ teaspoon chilli powder	½ tablespoon salt

Preparation
Coarsely chop the ginger and spring onions. Blend in an electric blender together with the turmeric, coriander, cumin and chilli powder. Cut the fish into bite-size pieces. Cut the tomatoes into quarters.

Cooking

Heat the oil in a large heavy pan. Add the blended ingredients and stir-fry for 3 minutes. Add ½ cup of coconut milk, stir and add the fish. Continue to stir and simmer for 10 minutes. Add the quartered tomatoes, sugar and salt. Simmer until the fish is cooked, then serve immediately.

Laksa
Prawn and noodles

Serves 6 Cooking time 10 minutes

1 anchovy fillet	2 onions
peel of ½ lemon	¼ teaspoon saffron
2 fresh green chillies	1½ lb (750 g) cooked peeled prawns
2 teaspoons salt	4 tablespoons oil
½ teaspoon freshly ground pepper	2 cups coconut milk (see page 105)
½ cup cashew nuts	8 oz (250 g) vermicelli noodles
3 cloves garlic	

Preparation

In an electric blender, blend together the anchovy fillet, lemon peel, green chillies, salt, pepper, cashew nuts, garlic, onions and saffron with a little oil.

Cooking

Heat the remaining oil in a large pan. Add the blended ingredients and fry for 5 minutes, stirring continuously. Add the prawns and continue to fry for a further 2 minutes. Pour in the coconut milk and gently bring to the boil. Reduce the heat and simmer for 2 minutes. In a second saucepan, cook the vermicelli noodles until they are soft, drain and place on a large serving dish. Pour the prawns and sauce over the noodles and serve.

Ikan asam
Sour fish

Serves 6 Cooking time 20 minutes

1½ lb (750 g) white fish fillets (cod, bream, snapper)	3 in (7.5 cm) fresh root ginger
	½ cup blanched almonds

peel of ½ lemon
2 teaspoons turmeric
1 anchovy fillet
2 spring onions

4 fresh red chillies
3 tablespoons oil
juice of 2 lemons

Preparation

Cut the fish into thin strips. Chop the ginger and blend in an electric blender the ginger, almonds, lemon peel, turmeric, anchovy fillet, spring onions and red chillies with a little oil until you have a smooth paste.

Cooking

Heat the remaining oil in a large heavy pan. Add the blended ingredients and fry for 5 minutes. Add the lemon juice and 2 cups of water. Bring to the boil, reduce the heat and simmer for 10 minutes. Add the strips of fish and cook gently for 5 minutes. Remove the fish and place on a hot serving plate. Strain the cooking sauce, pour over the fish and serve.

Otak otak

Wrapped steamed fish

Note: Banana leaves are used daily to cook this dish in Malaysia, but aluminium foil is easily substituted.

Serves 4 Cooking time 35 minutes

2 cloves garlic
3 fresh green chillies
peel of ½ lemon
1 teaspoon turmeric
2 teaspoons salt

½ teaspoon freshly ground pepper
4 tablespoons desiccated coconut
1 cup coconut milk (see page 105)
4 large white fish fillets, total
  weight about 1½ lb (750 g)

Preparation

Put the garlic, green chillies, lemon peel, turmeric, salt, pepper, desiccated coconut and a little of the coconut milk into an electric blender. Blend until you have a smooth paste. Wash each fish fillet under cold running water and pat dry. Cut 4 pieces of aluminium foil large enough to wrap up each fillet. Cut each of the fillets into thin strips.

Cooking

Heat the remaining coconut milk in a saucepan. Do not let it boil. Remove from the heat and add the blended paste. Stir well. Lay out each sheet of foil on your work top. Spread some of the coconut paste on each. Place the strips of fillet on top and spread the remaining paste evenly over the four piles. Fold up the foil and seal to make 4 parcels. Place the parcels in a steamer and steam for 30 minutes. Serve straight from the wrappers.

Guleh ikan
Fish curry

Serves 6 Cooking time 40 minutes

2 lb (1 kg) fillets of sole	3 teaspoons sugar
2 teaspoons salt	1 tablespoon cornflour
3 onions	5 tablespoons oil
3 in (7.5 cm) fresh root ginger	1 teaspoon chilli powder
½ cup cashew nuts	¼ teaspoon saffron
juice of 1 lemon	2 cups coconut milk (see page 105)

Preparation

Cut the fillets into serving portions. Wash under cold running water, pat dry and sprinkle with the salt. Finely slice the onions. Mince the ginger and the cashew nuts. Blend together the lemon juice, sugar and cornflour.

Cooking

Heat 3 tablespoons of the oil in a large heavy pan and fry the fillets until they are golden brown. Remove and drain. Add the remaining oil to the pan and toss in the onions. Fry until they are just transparent. Remove about half the onions and put to one side. To the remaining onions, add the minced ginger and nuts together with the chilli powder, saffron and coconut milk. Bring gently to the boil. Pour in the blended cornflour, sugar and lemon juice, reduce the heat and return the fish to the pan. Simmer gently for 10 minutes. Remove the fish fillets and arrange on a serving plate. Pour over the sauce and garnish with the reserved onions.

Meat

Beef satay
Skewered beef

Serves 4-6 Cooking time 10 minutes

1 lb (500 g) beef steak
1 onion
2 cloves garlic
peel of ½ lemon
1 teaspoon ground cumin
1 teaspoon powdered ginger
1 tablespoon turmeric

½ teaspoon freshly ground black pepper
½ teaspoon salt
1 teaspoon sugar
2 tablespoons soy sauce
2 tablespoons oil

Preparation
Cut the beef into bite-size pieces. Chop the onion, garlic and lemon peel finely. Pound or blend all three together with the cumin, ginger and turmeric. Add the freshly ground black pepper, salt, sugar and soy sauce. Mix well. Toss in the meat and leave to marinate for at least 1 hour. Thread the meat on to skewers, just before you are ready to cook.

Cooking
Grill under a high heat until cooked, basting 2 or 3 times with the oil. Serve immediately with peanut sauce (see page 126), raw onion and cucumber.

Pork satay
Skewered pork

Serves 4 Cooking time 10 minutes

1 lb (500 g) pork fillet
3 onions
4 fresh red chillies
½ cup blanched almonds
2 cups coconut milk (see page 105)

4 tablespoons oil
2 teaspoons ground coriander
1 teaspoon salt
3 teaspoons sugar

Preparation
Cut the pork into small bite-size pieces. Coarsely chop the onions and the chillies and put them into an electric blender. Add the

almonds, coconut milk, oil, coriander, salt and sugar and blend until you have a smooth paste. Thread 3 or 4 pieces of the pork on to metal or bamboo skewers. Place the skewers in a shallow dish, pour over the paste and leave to marinate for 1 hour.

Cooking
Place under a hot grill and grill for 5 or 6 minutes on each side or cook on a charcoal fire. Serve at once.

Lamb satay
Skewered lamb

Serves 6 Cooking time 10 minutes

1 lb (500 g) lean lamb	1 teaspoon salt
4 cloves garlic	½ teaspoon pepper
3 tablespoons soy sauce	

Preparation
Cut the lamb into small bite-size pieces. Thread 3 or 4 on to metal or bamboo skewers. Finely chop the garlic and add the soy sauce, salt and pepper. Pour over the lamb *satays* and leave to marinate for 1 hour.

Cooking
Place under a hot grill and grill for 5 or 6 minutes on each side or cook on a charcoal fire. Serve at once.

Gulai kambing
Lamb curry

Serves 6 Cooking time 1¾ hours

1½ lb (750 g) lamb	1 teaspoon ground cumin
2 onions	1 teaspoon turmeric
4 cloves garlic	½ teaspoon cinnamon powder
2 tablespoons lemon juice	½ teaspoon nutmeg
1 in (2.5 cm) fresh root ginger	1 teaspoon freshly ground black
4 tablespoons desiccated coconut	pepper
2 tablespoons blanched almonds	2 tablespoons oil
4 dried red chillies	1 small can peeled tomatoes
peel of ¼ lemon	2 cups coconut milk (see page 105)
2 teaspoons ground coriander	2 teaspoons salt

Preparation

Cut the lamb into small bite-size pieces. Coarsely chop the onions and put into an electric blender with the garlic, lemon juice and ginger and blend into a smooth paste. Toast the coconut in a dry pan until just turning brown and add to your blended ingredients. Add the almonds, red chillies, lemon peel and all the spices to the blender. Blend once more until you have a smooth paste.

Cooking

Heat the oil in a large heavy saucepan and add the blended paste. Fry for 5 minutes, stirring constantly. Add the lamb and fry for 5 more minutes, stirring continuously. Add the tomatoes, coconut milk and salt and bring gently to the boil. Leave uncovered for 1½ hours, stirring occasionally. Serve.

Sambal babi
Spiced pork in coconut milk

Serves 6 Cooking time 1 hour 10 minutes

1½ lb (750 g) belly pork	1 teaspoon prawn paste
2 in (5 cm) fresh root ginger	2 teaspoons ground coriander
peel of 1 lemon	1 teaspoon ground cumin
2 onions	2 teaspoons sugar
4 cloves garlic	1 teaspoon salt
1½ cups coconut milk (see page 105)	2 teaspoons chilli powder
	1 teaspoon turmeric

Preparation

Cut the pork into small bite-size pieces. Grate the ginger and the lemon peel. Finely chop the onions. Crush and chop the garlic.

Cooking

Put all the ingredients into a large heavy saucepan. Bring gently to the boil, stirring continuously. Reduce the heat and continue to simmer for about 1 hour, by which time the pork will be tender and most of the liquid evaporated. Serve.

Poultry
Panggang golek
Spiced duck

Serves 4 Cooking time 1¾ hours

1 5-lb (2.5-kg) duck, with liver and giblets	2 teaspoons powdered ginger
3 large onions	2 cloves garlic
2 tablespoons ground coriander	½ cup peanuts
1 teaspoon cumin	½ teaspoon chilli powder
1 teaspoon turmeric	3 teaspoons salt
½ teaspoon anise	1½ cups coconut milk (see page 105)

Preparation

Wash and pat dry the duck. Prick the entire surface with a sharp knife. Chop the liver and giblets and place in an electric blender. Cut one of the onions into quarters. Add to the blender the coriander, cumin, turmeric, anise, powdered ginger, garlic, peanuts, chilli powder and the quartered onion. Blend all the ingredients until you have a thick paste. Finely chop the remaining onions. Put 3 tablespoons of the paste to one side.

Cooking

Place the remaining paste and the chopped onions into a pan over a moderate heat and add the salt and the coconut milk. Simmer gently for 15 minutes. Remove from the heat and leave to cool. When cool, stuff the duck with this mixture and sew or skewer the opening. Preheat the oven to hot, 425°F, 220°C or Gas Mark 7. Put the duck on a rack and place in the oven for 1½ hours or until it is cooked. During cooking, smear the skin once or twice with the paste you set aside. When cooked, carve and serve with the stuffing.

Opor
Spiced chicken

Serves 4 Cooking time 45 minutes

1 4-lb (2-kg) chicken	1 teaspoon cumin
2 tablespoons ground coriander	2 teaspoons cinnamon powder

½ teaspoon ground cloves
½ teaspoon ground cardamom
½ teaspoon ground nutmeg
2 teaspoons freshly ground pepper
2 teaspoons salt
2 onions

peel of ½ lemon
3 cloves garlic
2 tablespoons butter
2 tablespoons oil
2 cups desiccated coconut
1 cup coconut milk (see page 105)

Preparation

Cut the chicken into small serving portions. With a sharp knife, stab the surfaces of each piece. Mix together the coriander, cumin, cinnamon, cloves, cardamom, nutmeg, pepper and salt. Sprinkle this mixture of spices all over the chicken and leave to stand for 1 hour. Slice the onions and grate the lemon peel. Crush and chop the garlic.

Cooking

In a large saucepan, heat the butter and oil. Toss in the desiccated coconut and fry until it is just brown. Add the chicken and spices together with the sliced onions, the grated lemon peel and the chopped garlic. Pour in the coconut milk, cover and simmer gently over a very low heat for 40 minutes or until the chicken is quite tender. Serve.

Gulai ayam
Chicken curry

Serves 4   Cooking time 45 minutes

1 4-lb (2-kg) chicken
10 whole blanched almonds
3 tablespoons coriander seeds
1 teaspoon ground cumin
1 teaspoon fennel seeds
2 teaspoons cinnamon powder
3 whole cloves
12 small dried chillies

1 teaspoon turmeric
2 onions
peel of ½ lemon
5 tablespoons oil
½ teaspoon prawn paste
2 teaspoons salt
3½ cups coconut milk (see page 105)

Preparation

Cut the chicken into small serving portions. Put the almonds, coriander seeds, cumin, fennel seeds, cinnamon, cloves, dried chillies and the turmeric into an electric blender and grind into a fine powder. Finely slice the onions. Grate the lemon peel.

Cooking

Heat the oil in a large flameproof casserole. Add the spices, onions, grated lemon peel, prawn paste and the salt. Fry for 5 or 6 minutes, then add 2 or 3 tablespoons of the coconut milk. Stir so that you have a thick sauce. Add the chicken pieces and mix well to ensure they are well coated with the sauce. Add most of the remaining coconut milk (reserve about ½ cup), cover and simmer until the chicken is tender. Check from time to time to make sure the sauce does not dry up. If it does, add a little water. When cooked, pour in the last of the coconut milk, *do not stir,* and serve.

Vegetables

Sayur lotay
Mixed boiled vegetables

Serves 6 Cooking time 10 minutes

4 cabbage leaves		4 cloves garlic
1 large potato		2 large onions
12 French beans	or any other	5 tablespoons oil
1 carrot	combination	1 teaspoon chilli powder
1 small aubergine	of vegetables	3 cups coconut milk (see page 105)
1 green pepper		1 tablespoon sugar
		1 teaspoon salt

Preparation

Shred the cabbage. Chop the potato into small pieces. Slice the beans, carrot, aubergine and green pepper. Slice the garlic and onion very finely.

Cooking

Heat the oil in a deep pan. When hot, toss in the garlic and onions. Fry for 2 minutes, then add the chilli powder. Stir well. Add the sliced green pepper and fry for a few moments, then pour in about ½ cup of the coconut milk. Add the sugar and the salt and simmer for 1 minute before adding the other vegetables. Stir well, then pour in the remaining coconut milk. Bring to the boil, stirring continuously. Reduce the heat and simmer for 5 minutes, then serve.

Masak lemak
Curried cabbage

Serves 4 Cooking time 25 minutes

1 onion	1 teaspoon prawn paste
2 fresh red chillies	2 teaspoons turmeric
1 large potato	1½ cups coconut milk (see page
½ white cabbage	105)

Preparation
Finely slice the onion. Chop the red chillies. Peel and dice the potato. Shred the cabbage.

Cooking
Put the sliced onion, the chopped chillies, prawn paste, turmeric and half the coconut milk in a large heavy saucepan. Place over a moderate heat and bring to the boil. Reduce the heat to low, toss in the diced potato and leave to simmer for 10 minutes. Add the shredded cabbage and continue to cook for a further 5 minutes, then pour in the remaining coconut milk. Bring back to the boil and stir. Serve at once.

Sambals and sauces
Sambals
Every Malaysian meal is accompanied with *sambals* – small fiery dishes that add extra flavour to a meal.

Onion sambal

3 cloves garlic	3 teaspoons sugar
3 onions	2 tablespoons white wine vinegar

Crush and chop the garlic very finely. Finely slice the onions. Spread the garlic over the onion slices and sprinkle with the sugar. Pour over the vinegar and leave to marinate for at least 30 minutes before serving.

Chilli sambal

3 fresh red chillies
2 teaspoons salt

3 teaspoons sugar
2 tablespoons vinegar

Finely slice the red chillies and sprinkle with the salt and sugar. Pour over the vinegar, mix well and leave for 2 hours to marinate.

Peanut sauce

Serves 4-6 Cooking time 20 minutes

1 onion
3 cloves garlic
1 teaspoon chilli powder
2 tablespoons sugar

2 tablespoons oil
1 cup crunchy peanut butter
juice of ½ lemon
3 cups coconut milk (see page 105)

Preparation
Finely chop the onion and garlic. Pound both together with the chilli powder and sugar.

Cooking
Heat the oil in a small saucepan and add the pounded ingredients. Stir frequently and cook for 5 minutes. Add the peanut butter, lemon juice and coconut milk. Bring to the boil, reduce the heat and simmer, stirring continuously, for about 15 minutes or until the sauce thickens.

Desserts
Baked bananas

Serves 6 Cooking time 12 minutes

2 oz (50 g) butter
1 oz (25 g) sugar
2 in (5 cm) fresh root ginger
¼ teaspoon ground cloves

2 tablespoons orange juice
1 tablespoon lemon juice
6 bananas

Preparation
Cream the butter and sugar together. Grate the ginger. Add the ginger, cloves, orange and lemon juices to the butter and sugar and beat well. Grease a baking dish. Lay the bananas in and pour over the butter mixture. Preheat your oven to 375°F, 190°C or Gas Mark 5.

Cooking
Place the baking dish in the oven and bake for 12 minutes, by which time the sauce should be bubbling and the bananas tender. Remove and serve.

Sarikauga
Coconut custard

Serves 6 Cooking time 25 minutes

4 eggs
1½ cups sugar
pinch salt

2 cups coconut milk (see page 105)
1 tablespoon desiccated coconut

Preparation
Beat the eggs, sugar, and the pinch of salt until light and frothy. Add the coconut milk. Pour into individual bowls or one large bowl. Place in a shallow pan of hot water. Cover the custard with aluminium foil. Preheat the oven to 350°F, 175°C or Gas Mark 4.

Cooking
Put the pan with the bowl or bowls into the preheated oven and bake for 25 minutes or until the custard is set. Allow to cool and sprinkle with the coconut before serving.

Thailand

I've visited Thailand on three occasions. Bangkok is the Venice of the East. As a visitor, one must travel the klongs (canals) where lush green jungle dips into the water's edge and masses of people live and work.

The most colourful of all sites on such a tour are the famous floating markets. Here the herbs and spices, beef, chicken, lobsters, prawns, oysters, vegetables and fruits that go into the

Thai cooking pot are bought and sold from long, narrow boats. From many, you can eat a delicious peppered chicken portion called *kai yang*, which is grilled over a simple charcoal fire. I even enjoyed my first taste of a Thai raw fish dish, marinated in coconut milk and lime juice, which I bought at a floating eating house. It is so similar to the dishes found throughout the Pacific Islands that I often wondered who introduced it to whom.

After each visit to Thailand, two aspects of the country have seemed larger than life to me. Firstly, the traffic. In Bangkok, in particular, the density and noise has grown over the years, now reaching proportions unequalled anywhere else in the world.

Secondly, the food! Thai food is a rich experience of taste, aroma and colour. The fiery hot curries, the likes of which I haven't encountered even in India. The sweet and sour flavours of limes, lemons and sweet local herbs and heavy aromas wafting through the air, created by blends of chillies, fresh coriander and lemons. And the meals on the tables – a feast for the eyes!

Soups
Kaeng chud
Prawn and coconut soup

Serves 6 Cooking time 15 minutes

1 onion	½ teaspoon ground coriander
2 cloves garlic	1 teaspoon chilli powder
1 anchovy fillet	3 cups coconut milk (see page 105)
2 teaspoons raw sugar	2 cups double cream
1 tablespoon soy sauce	1½ lb (750 g) green prawns
½ teaspoon freshly ground pepper	peel of ½ lemon
2 teaspoons salt	

Preparation
Coarsely chop the onion and the garlic. Place in an electric blender with the anchovy fillet, sugar, soy sauce, pepper, salt, coriander and chilli powder and blend into a smooth paste. Pour into a saucepan and add the coconut milk and cream. Blend together. Peel and devein the prawns. Wash under cold running water and pat dry. Chop the prawns. Grate the lemon peel.

Cooking

Place the pan over a low heat for 10 minutes, then add the prawns and the grated lemon peel. Continue to heat gently for 5 minutes – do not let it boil – then serve.

Kaeng ho mai
Spareribs and bamboo shoots soup

Serves 6 Cooking time 1 hour 10 minutes

1 lb (500 g) pork spareribs	1 teaspoon ground coriander
1 can bamboo shoots	5 cups chicken stock
2 cloves garlic	1 teaspoon freshly ground pepper
1 onion	2 teaspoons salt
4 spring onions	3 teaspoons sugar

Preparation

Divide the spareribs and cut them with a heavy cleaver into small pieces. Drain the bamboo shoots and dice. Crush the garlic and finely chop the onion. Finely slice the spring onions.

Cooking

Heat the oil in a large saucepan. Add the crushed garlic, the onions and coriander and fry for 2 or 3 minutes. Add the pieces of sparerib and fry until they are brown. Add the stock and season with pepper, salt and sugar. Bring to the boil, reduce the heat and simmer for 45 minutes, by which time the meat will be tender. Strain and retain the soup, replace the spareribs and add the diced bamboo shoots. Continue to simmer for 5 minutes, then serve garnished with the sliced spring onions.

Seafood
Pla priu wan lhing
Ginger-spiced fish

Serves 6 Cooking time 15 minutes

6 large mushrooms	½ cup beer
1 cup plain flour	1 tablespoon olive oil

6 fillets of sole	2 tablespoons soy sauce
4 spring onions	3 teaspoons sugar
10 pieces crystallised ginger	2 teaspoons powdered ginger
1 cup oil	1 tablespoon cornflour
2 tablespoons vinegar	3 sprigs parsley

Preparation

Peel and remove the stems of the mushrooms, then slice them very finely. Sift the flour in a bowl and add the beer and olive oil. Beat together until you have a smooth batter. Clean the fish fillets under cold running water and pat dry. Finely chop the spring onions. Finely chop the crystallised ginger.

Cooking

Heat the oil in a large heavy pan. Dip the fillets into the batter and place them into the hot oil. Fry until they are golden brown and the fish is cooked, turning each fillet over only once. Drain thoroughly and place on a serving plate in a warm oven. Mix together the vinegar, soy sauce, sugar, crystallised ginger, powdered ginger and the spring onions. Pour into a small saucepan and place over a low heat. Mix the cornflour with a little water and blend into the sauce. Continue to stir until the sauce is thick, then pour over the fish and garnish with the parsley before serving.

Kam koong
Prawn salad

Serves 6 Cooking time 3 minutes

2 lb (1 kg) cooked peeled prawns	1 cup peanuts
2 onions	2 tablespoons oil
3 cloves garlic	1 cup coconut milk (see page 105)
1 green pepper	2 tablespoons soy sauce
1 apple	

Preparation

Cut the prawns into small bite-size pieces. Finely mince the onions and the garlic. Finely chop the green pepper. Peel, core and grate the apple. Chop the peanuts.

Cooking

Heat the oil in a small pan. Fry the minced onion and garlic for 3
minutes. Leave to cool for 5 minutes, then pour into a bowl. Add
the green pepper, apple, peanuts, coconut milk and soy sauce.
Put the prawns into a serving bowl and pour over the mixed
vegetables and sauce. Place in a refrigerator and chill thoroughly
for 1 hour or more before serving.

Tord mun kung
Prawn balls

Serves 6 Cooking time 10 minutes

1 lb (500 g) green prawns	1 teaspoon salt
4 cloves garlic	2 cups dry breadcrumbs
½ teaspoon freshly ground black pepper	peanut oil for deep-frying

Preparation

Peel and devein the prawns. Wash them under cold running
water and pat dry. Mince the prawns with the garlic. Add the
freshly ground black pepper and the salt and mix thoroughly.
Shape into small balls and roll in the breadcrumbs.

Cooking

Heat the oil in a large deep saucepan and deep-fry the prawn
balls until they are cooked and golden brown. Drain thoroughly
and serve.

Meat

Kaeng phet nua
Beef curry

Serves 4 Cooking time 45 minutes

1 lb (500 g) rump steak	peel of ½ lemon
½ cup peanuts	2 teaspoons salt
4 spring onions	3½ cups coconut milk (see page 105)
3 cloves garlic	1 lb (500 g) spinach
2 in (5 cm) fresh root ginger	1 fresh red chilli

2 teaspoons raw sugar   1 cup yoghurt
1 teaspoon soy sauce

Preparation
Slice the steak into very thin strips. Mince the peanuts coarsely.
Blend in an electric blender the spring onions, garlic, ginger,
lemon peel, salt and a little of the coconut milk. When thoroughly
smooth, add a cup of coconut milk and blend into a sauce. Wash
and shred the spinach. Finely slice the red chilli.

Cooking
Heat the remaining coconut milk in a large heavy pan. Add the
strips of steak and bring to the boil. Reduce the heat and simmer
for 10 minutes. Add the minced peanuts to the pan along with the
sugar and soy sauce. Leave to simmer for a further 20 minutes.
Pour the blended sauce into a second large heavy pan and place
over a moderate heat. Cover tightly and simmer for 5 minutes.
Now pour the contents of the first pan into the second and return
to the boil. Reduce the heat, cover and leave to simmer until the
meat is tender. In the meantime, boil the spinach in salted water
for 3 minutes, drain thoroughly and make a bed on a large
serving plate. When the beef is tender and the sauce reduced,
pour on top of the spinach and garnish with the yoghurt and the
slices of red chilli before serving.

Ma ho
Pork stuffed oranges

Serves 6 Cooking time 25 minutes

1 lb (500 g) lean pork   2 teaspoons ground coriander
2 cloves garlic   1 teaspoon chilli powder
2 tablespoons peanuts   1 teaspoon nuoc mam (see page 155)
6 oranges   1 teaspoon salt
2 tablespoons oil

Preparation
Mince the pork very finely. Mince the garlic. Finely chop the
peanuts. Cut the oranges in half and scoop out most of the flesh.
Preheat the oven to 350°F, 175°C or Gas Mark 4.

Cooking

Heat the oil in a large heavy pan. Toss in the garlic and fry for 1 minute, add the minced pork, peanuts, coriander, chilli powder, nuoc mam and the salt. Stir-fry gently for 12 minutes. Stuff the pork mixture into the orange halves, place in the pre-heated oven and bake for 10 minutes.

Kaeng tom yam
Stuffed pork

Serves 6-8 Cooking time 3 hours 35 minutes

1 small leg of pork	2 teaspoons freshly ground black
2 cloves garlic	pepper
2 teaspoons ground coriander	1 lemon
1 tablespoon soy sauce	4 cups chicken stock
1 tablespoon nuoc mam (see page 155)	1 teaspoon chilli powder
	1 tablespoon cornflour
3 teaspoons salt	

Preparation

Have your butcher bone the pork for you. Make sure you have a nice deep pocket in the meat. Cut away all the scrappy ends of meat. You should have at least 1 lb (500 g). Mince this very finely with the garlic. Add to this the coriander, soy sauce, nuoc mam and freshly ground black pepper. Mix all together and stuff into the pocket. Sew up the gap. Rub the salt all over the surface of the meat. Cut the lemon into 6 pieces.

Cooking

Heat the oil in a very large deep pan or flameproof casserole. Add the meat and fry, turning it over several times, until all surfaces are browned. Pour in the chicken stock, add the lemon slices and the chilli powder. Cover, reduce the heat and simmer for 3½ hours, by which time the pork should be tender. Strain the cooking juices and thicken with the cornflour mixed with a little water. Slice the pork into thick pieces and pour the sauce over the meat.

Nua tang
Sweet mince

Serves 4 Cooking time 18 minutes

8 oz (250 g) pork
8oz (250 g) prawns
1 fresh red chilli
1½ cups coconut milk (see page 105)

2 teaspoons sugar
½ teaspoon freshly ground black pepper
1 teaspoon salt

Preparation
Finely mince the pork and prawns together. Finely slice the red chilli.

Cooking
Bring the coconut milk to a gentle boil. Add the minced pork and prawns. When the meat is cooked, in about 15 minutes, add the sugar, freshly ground black pepper, salt and the chilli. Simmer for 1 or 2 more minutes, then pour into bowls and serve.

Nua pad prik
Chilli beef

Serves 6 Cooking time 15 minutes

1½ lb (750 g) rump steak
1 teaspoon freshly ground black pepper
2 teaspoons salt

3 cloves garlic
3 fresh red chillies
2 sprigs parsley
2 tablespoons oil
2 tablespoons sugar

Preparation
Trim off the excess fat and cut the meat into large bite-size pieces. Sprinkle with the freshly ground black pepper and salt. Crush the garlic. Slice the red chillies. Chop the parsley.

Cooking
Heat the oil in a large heavy pan. Toss in the crushed garlic and fry for 2 minutes. Add the meat and fry until it is brown. Add the sliced chillies and sugar. Continue to stir-fry on a low heat for 5 minutes. Add the chopped parsley, stir and serve.

Poultry

Kai p'anaeng
Coconut and peanut chicken

Serves 6 Cooking time 25 minutes

1 onion	2 teaspoons sugar
2 cloves garlic	1 teaspoon salt
½ cup peanuts	2½ cups coconut milk (see page
2 teaspoons ground coriander	105)
1 teaspoon chilli powder	6 chicken breasts
peel of ½ lemon	2 tablespoons oil
	1 tablespoon soy sauce

Preparation
Cut the onion into quarters and place in an electric blender. Add the garlic, peanuts, coriander, chilli, lemon peel, sugar, salt and a little of the coconut milk and blend to a smooth paste. Place the chicken breasts in a bowl and coat with the paste and leave to marinate for 1 hour.

Cooking
Heat the oil in a large heavy pan and add the chicken breasts. Fry for 2 or 3 minutes or until the chicken is brown. Pour in the remaining coconut milk and the remaining marinade. Add the soy sauce, cover and simmer for 20 minutes. When the chicken is cooked and the sauce is thick, serve.

Kia chem pria wan
Sweet and spicy chicken

Serves 6 Cooking time 45 minutes

1 3-lb (1.5-kg) chicken	3 tablespoons sugar
2 cloves garlic	1½ tablespoons vinegar
2 onions	4 tablespoons oil
4 tomatoes	12 whole coriander seeds
2 green peppers	1 tablespoon water
½ small cucumber	2 tablespoons soy sauce
1 tablespoon cornflour	1 teaspoon salt
	½ teaspoon pepper

Preparation

Disjoint the chicken. Finely chop the garlic. Finely slice the onions. Cut the tomatoes into quarters. Coarsely chop the green peppers. Peel and dice the cucumber. Mix the cornflour, sugar and vinegar into a smooth paste.

Cooking

Heat the oil in a large pan. Add the chopped garlic and fry for 1 minute. Add the chicken pieces and brown well on all sides. Reduce the heat, cover and cook for 20 minutes. Add the onions, tomatoes, green peppers, cucumber and coriander seeds. Pour in the vinegar mixture and 1 tablespoon of water. Add the soy sauce, salt and pepper, stir and continue to cook for 5 minutes. Serve.

Kai tom kha
Chilli chicken

Serves 6   Cooking time 25 minutes

6 chicken breasts	peel of $\frac{1}{2}$ lemon
2 teaspoons salt	$2\frac{1}{2}$ cups coconut milk (see page
1 teaspoon freshly ground black	105)
pepper	3 teaspoons ground coriander
2 fresh red chillies	1 tablespoon soy sauce
	1 tablespoon lemon juice

Preparation

Cut the chicken breasts into small bite-size pieces. Sprinkle with the salt and freshly ground black pepper. Slice the red chillies. Grate the lemon peel.

Cooking

Put the chicken into a saucepan and pour in $1\frac{1}{2}$ cups of coconut milk. Bring to boiling point, reduce the heat, cover and leave to simmer for 20 minutes. Add the sliced chillies and the grated lemon peel. Pour in the remaining coconut milk and sprinkle with the coriander. At the last minute, add the soy sauce and lemon juice, stir well and serve.

Kai tord
Fried chicken

Serves 6 Cooking time 10 minutes

6 cloves garlic
2 teaspoons freshly ground black
  pepper
1 small onion

1 sprig parsley
oil for deep-frying
6 chicken breasts

Preparation
Blend in an electric blender the garlic, freshly ground black
pepper, onion and parsley with a little oil until you have a smooth
paste. Coat the chicken breasts with this paste and leave for 1
hour.

Cooking
Heat the remaining oil in a deep pan or wok. Drop in the coated
chicken breasts and deep-fry until golden brown. Drain thoroughly before serving.

Vegetables
Kayanthi hmat
Stuffed aubergines

Serves 6 Cooking time 45 minutes

3 medium-sized aubergines
4 teaspoons salt
8 oz (250 g) cooked peeled prawns
2 chicken breasts
2 cloves garlic

2 onions
3 sprigs parsley
1 teaspoon chilli powder
2 teaspoons turmeric
2 tablespoons oil

Preparation
Cut the aubergines, lengthwise, in half. Scoop out most of the
flesh. Chop the flesh quite finely. Sprinkle with half the salt and
put to one side to drain. Sprinkle the remaining salt into the
aubergine halves and turn them upside down on to kitchen paper
for 5 minutes. In the meantime, finely chop the prawns. Cut the
flesh from the chicken breasts and chop. Finely chop the garlic

and onions. Chop the parsley. Mix together the drained chopped aubergines, the prawns, chicken, garlic, onions and parsley. Season with the chilli powder and turmeric. Pour in the oil and mix all together. Drain and wipe the aubergines. Fill them with the mixed ingredients. Preheat the oven to 375°F, 190°C or Gas Mark 5.

Cooking
Place the stuffed aubergines into the preheated oven and bake for 45 minutes. Serve.

Desserts
Khan om kluk
Coconut pancakes

Serves 6 Cooking time 15 minutes

1 cup rice flour	3 eggs
1 cup sugar	1 tablespoon oil
¼ teaspoon salt	½ cup desiccated coconut
2 cups coconut milk (see page 105)	

Preparation
Sift the flour, sugar and salt. Pour in the coconut milk and add the eggs. Beat thoroughly until you have a smooth batter.

Cooking
Heat a few drops of the oil in a small pan. Pour in enough batter just to coat the bottom. Brown on one side before turning over. Brown on the second, then roll the pancake up and keep warm. Repeat until all have been cooked. Sprinkle with the coconut and serve with cream.

Mok si kao
Coconut cakes

Serves 6 Cooking time 15 minutes

2 cups rice flour	2 ripe bananas
1 egg	½ cup raw sugar
2 teaspoons baking powder	oil for deep-frying
1 cup desiccated coconut	

Preparation
Blend together the rice flour, egg, baking powder and coconut into a smooth, lump-free paste. Slice the bananas. Dissolve the sugar in a little water over a moderate heat, then pour into the flour paste. Beat thoroughly into a smooth batter. Leave to stand for 30 minutes. Add the sliced bananas.

Cooking
Heat the oil in a deep pan and drop in, one at a time, tablespoons of the batter. Fry until golden brown. Remove and drain thoroughly. Leave to cool before serving.

Vietnam

It is a pity that, because of war and political upheavals, I have never been able to visit Vietnam and learn from the locals how to prepare their food. However, I have now received valuable tuition from many beautiful and helpful Vietnamese cooks, who have arrived as refugees in both Australia and the United Kingdom, after perilous escape journeys across the South China Sea.

These charming people have spent many hours with me in their new homes, often with an interpreter, explaining their ingredients and demonstrating their cooking skills.

The most obvious tradition of the Vietnamese cooks is similar in many respects to her Thai and Japanese counterparts. Food must be beautifully presented. Much time and care is taken to arrange salads decoratively, meats are fanned out on beds of lettuce, and vegetables are carved. These skills are taught to the women as young girls – and now they will spend hours in the kitchen preparing every evening meal.

One snack meal, which is served in many markets and street stalls in Vietnam, illustrates the artistry of the cooks as much as any other. *Chao tom* is a piece of peeled sugar cane, about six inches long. Around the centre is moulded minced prawns and herbs which are then roasted over a charcoal fire. It is a masterpiece of culinary skill, beautiful to the eye and scrumptious to eat.

Starters and snacks
Bahn mi chien tom
Prawn toast

Serves 6 Cooking time 15 minutes

6 slices stale bread	¼ small cucumber
12 larged cooked peeled prawns	6 lettuce leaves
1 tablespoon butter	6 teaspoons nuoc mam (see page
1 teaspoon oil	155)
½ teaspoon salt	24 mint leaves
½ teaspoon freshly ground pepper	oil for frying

Preparation
Cut the crusts off the bread. Blend in an electric blender the prawns, butter, oil, salt and pepper to a smooth paste. Spread the paste on to the slices of bread. Peel and slice the cucumber.

Cooking
Heat the oil in a deep pan. Put the slices of bread, paste side down, into the hot oil, 1 or 2 slices at a time. Fry until golden brown. Drain on kitchen paper. Slice diagonally into quarters. Place a lettuce leaf on each plate and arrange the 4 quarters on top with a teaspoon of nuoc mam for dipping and the cucumber slices as an accompaniment. Garnish with the mint leaves.

Tom vo vien
Prawn cakes

Serves 4 Cooking time 10 minutes

2 spring onions	1 teaspoon salt
1 lb (500 g) cooked peeled prawns	½ teaspoon freshly ground black
1 tablespoon nuoc mam (see page	pepper
155)	1 teaspoon flour
3 sprigs parsley	4 tablespoons oil

Preparation
Chop the spring onions and place in an electric blender with the
prawns, nuoc mam, parsley, salt and pepper. Blend to a smooth
paste. Sprinkle the flour on to a board and form the paste into
small flat cakes. When they are all made, put into the refrigerator
and chill for 30 minutes.

Cooking
Heat the oil in a large heavy pan. Add the cakes, a few at a time,
and fry on one side until golden brown. Turn over and brown the
other side. Remove and drain on kitchen paper. Serve hot.

Cha gio
Spring rolls

Serves 6 Cooking time 15 minutes

8 oz (250 g) crabmeat (fresh or canned)	3 cups bean sprouts (fresh or
1 spring onion	canned)
1 egg	12 spring roll wrappers (frozen)
1 carrot	oil for deep-frying

Preparation
Flake the crabmeat and place in a bowl. Chop the spring onion,
grate the carrot and chop the bean sprouts. Put all three into a
bowl with the crabmeat. Beat the egg and add to the crabmeat
and vegetables. Mix all together thoroughly. Put about 2 tablespoons into the centre of each spring roll wrapper. Spread it out
diagonally across the centre. Roll up, starting from one corner
opposite the pile of filling. Fold in the two side corners to seal

completely. Dampen down the last corner with a little water to seal as you finally roll it up.

Cooking
Heat the oil in a deep pan. Carefully put the spring rolls into the hot oil and deep-fry until they are golden brown. Remove from the oil and drain on kitchen paper. Serve hot.

Trung chien voi Cua
Crab omelette

Serves 4 Cooking time 6 minutes

4 eggs	4 spring onions
1 teaspoon salt	1 fresh red chilli
½ teaspoon pepper	1 tablespoon oil
4 oz (125 g) crabmeat (fresh or canned)	1 teaspoon nuoc mam (see page 155)

Preparation
Beat the eggs and season with the salt and pepper. Flake the crabmeat. Chop the spring onions. Finely slice the red chilli.

Cooking
Heat half the oil in a pan and add the onions and chilli. Fry for 1 or 2 minutes. Add the crab and the nuoc mam. Stir well and remove. Clean the pan and return it to the heat. Add the remaining oil and pour in the beaten eggs. Cook until set on the bottom but still creamy on top. Spoon the crab mixture down the centre of the omelette and fold in half. Leave for 1 minute, then remove, cut into 4 and serve.

Soups
Canh chua ga
Chicken and pineapple soup

Serves 4 Cooking time 12 minutes

1 small can pineapple pieces
1 chicken breast
½ green pepper
2 sticks celery
4 mint leaves

3 cups chicken stock (see page 83)
2 tablespoons nuoc mam (see page 155)
2 teaspoons sugar
juice of ½ lemon

Preparation
Drain the pineapple. Remove the flesh from the chicken breast and cut the meat into small pieces. Cut the pepper and celery into small bite-size pieces. Coarsely chop the mint leaves.

Cooking
Bring the chicken stock to the boil and add the chicken vegetables and the pineapple. Reduce the heat and simmer for 5 minutes, then add the nuoc mam, sugar and lemon juice. Continue to simmer for 5 more minutes, then serve garnished with the mint leaves.

Pho
Beef and noodle soup

Serves 6 Cooking time 2 hours 20 minutes

2 onions
2 cloves garlic
12 oz (750 g) stewing beef
2 small veal bones
8 cups water
2 teaspoons salt
½ teaspoon freshly ground pepper

1 teaspoon nuoc mam (see page 155)
1 teaspoon vinegar
1 cup flour
1 tablespoon warm water
1 egg

Preparation
Coarsely chop the onions. Crush and chop the garlic.

Cooking

Place the meat in a large saucepan. Add the bones, chopped onions, garlic, the water, salt and pepper. Place over a medium heat and boil gently for 2 hours. Strain and retain the soup. Put the meat to one side. Add the nuoc mam and vinegar. Return to the heat and continue to simmer. Quickly mix together the flour, warm water and the egg, until you have a smooth dough. Knead for 1 or 2 minutes, then force through the holes of a colander or squeeze through a potato masher straight into the boiling soup. Continue to cook for 10 minutes or until the noodles are tender. In the meantime, cut up the meat into bite-size pieces and return to the soup. Serve.

Seafood

Goi Tom
Prawn and chicken salad

Serves 6

8 oz (250 g) carrots
1 cucumber
4 stalks celery
2 cooked chicken breasts
8 oz (250 g) cooked peeled prawns
1 teaspoon anchovy sauce

1 tablespoon vinegar
3 teaspoons sugar
½ teaspoon chilli powder
½ cup peanuts
8 mint leaves
2 sprigs parsley

Preparation

Peel and thinly slice the carrots lengthwise, then cut into thin strips. Peel and cut the cucumber into similar size strips. Dice the celery. Shred the flesh from the chicken breasts. Crush and finely chop the garlic and add to it the anchovy sauce, vinegar, sugar and chilli powder. Crush the peanuts. Mix the carrots, cucumber and celery together with the garlic and anchovy sauce mixture. Place on a serving dish and top with the prawns, chicken and peanuts. Garnish with the mint and parsley.

Muc xao chua ngot
Sweet and sour squid

Serves 4 Cooking time 10 minutes

8 oz (250 g) squid (calamari)
4 oz (125 g) broccoli
1 onion
2 in (5 cm) fresh root ginger
½ cup chicken stock
1 tablespoon vinegar
1 tablespoon sugar

2 teaspoons cornflour
1 tablespoon soy sauce
1 tablespoon nuoc mam (see page 155)
2 tablespoons oil
4 sprigs parsley

Preparation

Thoroughly wash the squid under cold running water. Stab with a sharp knife all over the surface. Cut into small bite-size pieces. Cut the broccoli into bite-size pieces. Slice the onion. Cut the ginger into matchstick-size pieces. Mix together the stock, vinegar, sugar, cornflour, soy sauce and nuoc mam.

Cooking

Heat the oil in a large heavy pan. Add the onions and ginger. Fry for 3 or 4 minutes, then add the squid and broccoli and fry for a further 2 minutes, stirring occasionally. Pour in the blended sauce and stir until the sauce thickens. Pour into a serving bowl and garnish with the sprigs of parsley.

Moke khat pa
Steamed fish

Serves 6 Cooking time 1 hour

2 lb (1 kg) mackerel fillets
8 oz (250 g) green prawns
2 teaspoons chilli sauce
1 teaspoon nuoc mam (see page 155)

3 spring onions
2 cloves garlic
½ teaspoon salt

Preparation

Cut the fish into bite-size pieces, removing any bones or skin. Peel and devein the prawns. Wash under cold running water and pat dry. Chop them and mix together with the fish. Add the chilli sauce and nuoc mam. Chop the spring onions and garlic and add together with the salt. Mix well. Cut kitchen foil into 6 pieces, each 12 in by 8 in (30 cm by 20 cm). Place some of the mixture in the centre of each piece. Fold over the foil into envelope-shaped packets and seal.

Cooking
Place the 6 packets in a steamer over boiling water and steam for 1 hour, then remove and serve.

Tom kho tau
Fried prawns and spring onion

Serves 4 Cooking time 10 minutes

15 spring onions	3 teaspoons sugar
1 lb (500 g) green prawns	1 tablespoon nuoc mam (see page 155)
4 tablespoons oil	sprigs of mint

Preparation
Chop the spring onions into fairly long pieces of about 1 in (2.5 cm). Peel and devein the prawns but leave the heads and tails on. Wash under cold running water and pat dry.

Cooking
Heat the oil in a large heavy pan and fry the prawns and spring onions for 4 minutes. Add the nuoc mam and sugar and stir for 3 more minutes. Serve and garnish with sprigs of mint.

Yam
Prawn and pork salad

Serves 6

2 cloves garlic	1 teaspoon freshly ground pepper
8 oz (250 g) cold roast pork	3 tablespoons wine vinegar
½ small cucumber	2 tablespoons lemon juice
6 mint leaves	½ teaspoon chilli powder
1 teaspoon ground coriander	1 lb (500 g) cooked peeled prawns
	4 small red chillies

Preparation

Mince the garlic. Cut the roast pork into small bite-size pieces. Peel and slice the cucumber. Finely chop the mint. Mix together the minced garlic, coriander, pepper, vinegar, lemon juice and chilli powder. Toss in the pork, prawns and cucumber. Garnish with the chopped mint, the chillies, chill and serve.

Cua rang muoi
Pepper crab

Serves 6 Cooking time 15 minutes

6 uncooked crabs	6 cloves garlic
2 tablespoons salt	4 teaspoons black peppercorns
1 fresh red chilli	3 tablespoons oil
6 spring onions	

Preparation

Cut the crabs into serving portions. Remove all the inedible parts. Crack the claws. Place all the pieces in a large bowl. Mix the salt with water until it dissolves, then pour over the crabs. Top up with more water so that the crabs are completely covered. Leave for 30 minutes. In the meantime, finely slice the red chilli, chop the spring onions and crush the garlic. Bruise the peppercorns and put to one side. Drain the crabs.

Cooking

Heat the oil in a very large pan or wok and fry the garlic for 1 or 2 minutes. Add all the crab and fry for 5 minutes. Add the spring onions and peppercorns and continue to fry until the crabs are cooked. Place on a serving plate and garnish with the sliced chilli.

Meat

Thit heo kho tieu
Caramel pork

Serves 6 Cooking time 1½ hours

2 lb (1 kg) belly pork
3 cloves garlic
4 tablespoons sugar
1 cup water
1 teaspoon freshly ground pepper

1 tablespoon salt
2 tablespoons nuoc mam (see page 155)
2 tablespoons honey
3 cups boiling water

Preparation
Cut the pork into small bite-size pieces. Crush and chop the garlic. Put the sugar into a small saucepan over a medium heat. As it starts to caramelise, carefully start to add the 1 cup of water and stir. When all the water is added, leave to simmer for 1 minute, then put to one side to cool. Add the crushed garlic, pepper, salt, nuoc mam and honey. Mix well together, then rub into the pieces of pork. Leave to marinate for 3 hours.

Cooking
Put the meat and marinade into a flameproof casserole or a deep saucepan and pour in the boiling water. Place over a low heat and simmer for 1½ hours. Serve when the pork is tender and the sauce is really thick.

Thit Kho to
Pork with soy sauce

Serves 4 Cooking time 2 hours

1 lb (500 g) belly pork
4 cloves garlic
8 spring onions

2 in (5 cm) fresh root ginger
4 tablespoons soy sauce
2 teaspoons freshly ground pepper

Preparation
Cut the pork into serving portions. Finely chop the garlic and the spring onions. Grate the ginger.

Cooking

Put the pork, garlic, onions and ginger in a deep pan. Cover with water and place over a medium heat. Bring to the boil, reduce the heat and simmer for 2 hours. Remove and drain. Sprinkle with the soy sauce and pepper and serve.

Thit bo kho
Stewed beef

Serves 6 Cooking time 2 hours

1½ lb (750 g) stewing beef	2 teaspoons salt
10 mint leaves	3 tablespoons oil
1 in (2.5 cm) fresh root ginger	2 teaspoons ground coriander
6 spring onions	1 teaspoon ground cumin
1 tablespoon nuoc mam (see page 155)	1 teaspoon turmeric
	½ teaspoon chilli powder
1 teaspoon freshly ground pepper	

Preparation

Cut the meat into small bite-size pieces. Chop the mint leaves. Grate the ginger. Shred the spring onions. Mix together the meat with the chopped mint, nuoc mam, pepper and salt and leave to marinate for 20 minutes.

Cooking

Heat the oil in a large heavy pan, add the meat and marinade and fry until meat is brown. Add the ginger and spices to the pan. Continue to fry for a further 5 minutes, then pour in enough water just to cover the meat. Cover and bring to the boil, reduce the heat and simmer over a low heat for 1½ hours or until the meat is tender and the gravy is thick. Serve in a serving bowl, and garnish with the shredded spring onions.

Bo xao mang
Steak and bamboo shoots

Serves 6 Cooking time 12 minutes

1 lb (500 g) rump steak	4 tablespoons oil
1 large can bamboo shoots	1 tablespoon nuoc mam (see page
8 spring onions	155)
2 cloves garlic	½ teaspoon salt
6 tablespoons sesame seeds	

Preparation
Cut the steak into very thin strips. Drain and slice the bamboo
shoots. Finely slice the spring onions. Crush the garlic. Toast the
sesame seeds in a dry pan until they start to pop, then crush and
put to one side.

Cooking
Put half the oil into a large heavy pan or wok. Add the steak and
stir-fry for 2 minutes, then remove and put to one side. Add the
remaining oil to the wok and toss in the bamboo shoots, garlic
and spring onions. Stir-fry for 2 minutes. Pour in the nuoc nam
and sprinkle with the salt. Fry for 5 more minutes, then return the
steak and continue to cook for 3 or 4 more minutes. Sprinkle with
the crushed sesame seeds and mix together. Serve.

Poultry
Ga hap ca
Steamed chicken and tomatoes

Serves 4 Cooking time 30 minutes

4 chicken breasts	½ teaspoon chilli powder
4 tomatoes	1 teaspoon salt
4 spring onions	½ teaspoon freshly ground pepper
1 in (2.5 cm) fresh root ginger	1 teaspoon sugar
2 tablespoons nuoc mam (see page	2 teaspoons oil
155)	

Preparation

Bone the chicken and cut all the flesh into bite-size pieces. Cut the tomatoes into quarters. Finely chop the spring onions and grate the ginger. Put all the ingredients into a casserole and mix together.

Cooking

Place the casserole into a deep saucepan and pour enough water into the saucepan to come halfway up the casserole. Put a lid on the casserole and one on the saucepan. Place over a high heat and steam for 30 minutes or until the chicken is tender. Serve.

Ga xao xa ot
Lemon chicken

Serves 4 Cooking time 15 minutes

1 2½-lb (1.25-kg) chicken	1 cup peanuts
peel of 1 lemon	2 tablespoons oil
4 spring onions	2 teaspoons sugar
½ teaspoon salt	1 tablespoon nuoc mam (see page
½ teaspoon freshly ground pepper	155)
2 fresh red chillies	juice of ½ lemon

Preparation

Disjoint the chicken and cut into serving portions. Finely grate the lemon peel. Chop the spring onions. Mix together the chicken pieces, lemon peel and spring onions and season with the salt and pepper. Leave for 20 minutes. Finely chop the red chillies. Roast and crush the peanuts.

Cooking

Heat the oil in a wok or a large heavy pan. Toss in the chicken, lemon peel and onions and stir-fry for 5 minutes. Add the chopped chillies and stir-fry for a further 5 minutes. Sprinkle with the sugar and add the peanuts. Pour in the nuoc mam and lemon juice and stir-fry for 5 more minutes, then serve.

Rice

Phoat khat
Mixed rice

Serves 6 Cooking time 45 minutes

10 spring onions	1½ cups long-grain rice
3 cloves garlic	4 cups chicken stock
1 lb (500 g) lean pork	2 teaspoons salt
4 oz (125 g) green prawns	1 teaspoon pepper
2 eggs	1 teaspoon powdered ginger
1 red pepper	2 tablespoons vinegar
2 tablespoons oil	

Preparation
Finely chop the spring onions. Mince the garlic. Cut the pork into small bite-size pieces. Peel and devein the prawns. Wash under cold running water and pat dry. Beat the eggs together. Cut the red pepper into thin julienne strips.

Cooking
Heat most of the oil in a large heavy pan. Add the spring onions and garlic. Fry for 1 or 2 minutes until they start to brown. Toss in the pork and prawns and fry for a further 5 minutes. Add the rice, stock, salt, pepper, powdered ginger and vinegar. Cover and reduce the heat to very low and leave to simmer for 30 minutes, or until the pork is cooked and the rice is tender.

In a second pan, use the remaining oil to make 2 omelettes out of the beaten eggs. Roll them together like a swiss roll and slice through to make long thin strips. When the rice is ready mix in the omelette strips and garnish with the strips of red pepper.

Sauces

Nuoc mam
Chilli sauce

No Vietnamese meal is considered complete without this sauce.

2 red chillies
1 clove garlic
1 teaspoon sugar
1 tablespoon vinegar

1 tablespoon water
4 tablespoons fish sauce or prawn
   paste
peel of 1 lemon

Preparation
Remove the seeds from the red chillies. Put all the ingredients into an electric blender and blend until you have a smooth sauce.

Burma

The Burmese are delightful and softly spoken people. They are more interested in enjoying their days than pursuing the battle to accumulate wealth. Burma is a country very much unaffected by the pressures and tensions of the twentieth century and it is difficult to find much Western influence even in the capital, Rangoon.

The Burmese are Buddhist and every village has its own pagoda and *pongyi*, where the chief Buddhist monk plays an important part in the day-to-day life of a community. He receives food in the form of offerings to the gods and heads numerous festivals at which large and elaborate meals are planned and enjoyed.

It seems that Burma was populated by a succession of migration waves from the north, most coming from Mongolia. Large influxes of Indians were attracted to Burma for higher wages and opportunites to cultivate the fertile lowlands.

So, once again, we have a cuisine that is, derived from a variety of sources which were combined to produce what is, today, typical Burmese cuisine.

A true breakfast does not exist. Maybe some coffee and bread at daybreak, but the first meal is enjoyed between 9 a.m. and 11 a.m. Called *tiffen*, this meal usually consists of just one or two dishes. The main meal is eaten early in the evening – between 5 p.m. and 6 p.m. – and consists of rice, soup, salad, several curries and accompaniments. No hors d'oeuvres are eaten as they are considered detrimental to the taste and enjoyment of the meal.

Curry is at the heart of all Burmese meals. But they are quite different to the curry dishes of India. A Burmese cook blends together a paste of pounded onions, garlic, chillies, turmeric root and *ngapi* (prawn paste) and adds lemon grass and lemon juice. Indians, on the other hand, grind a collection of dried spices together for their curries.

The salads are far from the Western idea of a salad. Crisp and colourful combinations of cold meats, seafoods and vegetables are topped with delicious sauces based on *ngapi*.

Desserts are not served as these are considered unimportant. However, much of the plentiful fruit available is consumed throughout the day and at meals' end.

Starters and snacks
Thanhat
Cucumber salad

Serves 6 .Cooking time 10 minutes

2 cucumbers	8 tablespoons white wine vinegar
3 onions	4 tablespoons oil
6 cloves garlic	1 teaspoon turmeric
1½ teaspoons sesame seeds	2 teaspoons sugar

Preparation
Peel the cucumbers and cut into bite-size pieces. Finely slice the onions. Crush and chop the garlic.

Cooking
Toast the sesame seeds in a dry pan until they are just starting to pop. Place the cucumber in a saucepan and add half the vinegar, then just cover with water and simmer until the cucumber is just tender and turning transparent. Remove and drain. Heat half the oil in a heavy pan and fry the onions and garlic until they are golden brown – but don't let them burn. Drain thoroughly and put to one side. Heat the remaining oil in a small saucepan. Add the turmeric, sugar and the remaining vinegar. Stir well and place over a low heat until all the sugar is dissolved. Put to one side and leave to cool. To assemble your salad, put the cucumber into a salad bowl, pour over the dressing, top with the brown onion and garlic and, finally, sprinkle with the sesame seeds.

Soups
Hincho
Vegetable soup

Serves 6 Cooking time 20 minutes

2 cloves garlic	8 oz (250 g) pumpkin
1 onion	1 large carrot
4 oz (125 g) green prawns	1 teaspoon pepper
½ small cabbage	2 teaspoons salt
8 oz (250 g) courgettes	6 cups chicken stock

Preparation

Crush the garlic and finely chop the onion. Peel and devein the prawns. Wash under cold running water and pat dry. Shred the cabbage. Thinly slice the courgettes. Cut the pumpkin into small cubes. Cut the carrot into matchstick pieces.

Cooking

Heat the stock in a large heavy saucepan. Add the garlic, onions, prawns, pepper and salt. Bring to the boil and add the cabbage, courgettes, pumpkin and carrot. Simmer for 15 minutes, then serve.

Hsan byoke
Fish soup

Serves 6 Cooking time 1 hour 5 minutes

2 lb (1 kg) whole fish (mackerel, sea bass)	2 stalks celery
3 tablespoons soy sauce	2 teaspoons salt
2 teaspoons freshly ground pepper	1 onion
¼ heart of cabbage	8 cups water
	4 tablespoons long-grain rice

Preparation

Fillet the fish. Retain the heads and bones. Cut the fillets into bite-size pieces. Place in a bowl and pour on the soy sauce and sprinkle with the pepper. Mix well and leave to marinate for 30 minutes. Shred the cabbage and dice the celery.

Cooking

Place the retained heads and bones in a large saucepan with the salt and onion. Pour in the water and place over a moderate heat. Bring to the boil and leave for 30 minutes. Remove and strain. Retain the stock and bring back to the boil. Add the rice and boil for 15 minutes. Add the fish and marinade and continue to simmer for a further 15 minutes. Add the vegetables and cook 5 more minutes, then serve.

Seafood

Nga baung doke
Steamed fish

Serves 4 Cooking time 25 minutes

2 lb (1 kg) fillets of sole	4 tablespoons desiccated coconut
2 teaspoons salt	½ teaspoon chilli powder
1 teaspoon turmeric	1 teaspoon flour
3 onions	3 tablespoons double cream
3 cloves garlic	1 tablespoon oil
1 in (2.5 cm) fresh root ginger	

Preparation
Rub the salt and the turmeric into the fish fillets. Coarsely chop the onions, garlic and ginger and place in an electric blender. Add the desiccated coconut, chilli powder, flour and a little water and blend all the ingredients into a paste. Add the cream and stir well. Place a large piece of aluminium foil on your working top. Smear it well with the oil. In the centre put some of your blended mixture, spreading it out to the size of one of the fillets. Place the fillet on top. Spread some paste on top of the fillet and continue to build up the pile using all the fillets. If it gets too high, make a second pile by the side of the first. Pour the remaining paste over the top. Fold up the sides of the foil and seal.

Cooking
Place the foil packet on a rack over water in a large saucepan or steamer. Make sure the water does not enter through the foil. Cover tightly and bring to the boil. Steam for 25 minutes, then serve.

Nga hin
Fish curry

Serves 4 Cooking time 25 minutes

4 8-oz (250-g) trout	4 cloves garlic
2 teaspoons salt	2 in (5 cm) fresh root ginger
1 teaspoon turmeric	2 fresh red chillies
5 tablespoons vinegar	5 tablespoons oil
3 onions	1 cup water

Preparation

Clean the fish thoroughly leaving the heads and tails on. With a sharp knife score each fish several times on each side. Mix together the salt and turmeric and rub into the flesh of each fish. Place the fish in a shallow flat dish and pour on the vinegar. Leave to marinate for 1 hour, turning the fish over once during this period. In the meantime, finely slice the onions. Finely chop the garlic, ginger and red chillies, then pound or blend together into a paste. Put to one side.

Cooking

In a large heavy pan, heat the oil. Toss in the onions and fry for a few minutes until they start to become transparent. Add the blended mixture and continue to fry for a further 3 minutes. Remove the fish from the marinade, discard the marinade and place the fish gently in the pan. Pour in the water and leave to simmer for about 10 to 15 minutes or until the fish is cooked and comes easily off the bone. Carefully lift out each fish and place on a serving plate. Pour the cooking sauce over the fish and serve at once.

Ne myit hin
Prawn and bamboo shoot curry

Serves 4 Cooking time 15 minutes

6 cloves garlic	3 sprigs parsley
2 onions	1 teaspoon turmeric
4 tablespoons oil	1 teaspoon ground coriander
8 oz (250 g) green prawns	1 teaspoon salt
1 can bamboo shoots	½ teaspoon pepper
2 fresh green chillies	1 cup boiling water
3 tomatoes	

Preparation

Crush the garlic, quarter the onions and place both in an electric blender with 1 tablespoon of oil and blend until you have a smooth paste. Peel and devein the prawns. Wash under cold running water and pat dry. Drain the bamboo shoots and cut into bite-size pieces. Slice the green chillies and coarsely chop the tomatoes. Chop the parsley.

Cooking

Heat the remaining oil in a large heavy pan. Add the blended onions and garlic along with the turmeric, coriander and the salt and pepper. Fry for 5 minutes, then add the prawns, sliced bamboo shoots, chillies and the chopped tomatoes. Stir well. Add the boiling water and simmer until the prawns are cooked and the sauce is thick. Garnish with the chopped parsley and serve.

Meat

Wey thani
Golden pork

Serves 6 Cooking time 2 hours

12 cloves garlic	2 tablespoons oil
3 onions	2 teaspoons salt
8 in (20 cm) fresh root ginger	2 tablespoons vinegar
3 lb (3.5 kg) belly pork	1 teaspoon chilli powder

Preparation

Crush and chop the garlic. Chop the onions. Peel and chop the ginger. Cut the pork into small bite-size pieces. In an electric blender, blend the garlic, onions, and ginger with a little of the oil to make a smooth paste. Strain the paste through a very fine sieve or cheesecloth and retain all the liquid.

Cooking

Put the retained liquid into a heavy saucepan with the pork and the remaining oil. Add the salt, vinegar and chilli powder and bring gently to the boil. Cover, reduce the heat and simmer for about 2 hours. Check to make sure it is not drying out – if it is, add a few tablespoons of water. When the pork is tender and golden brown in colour, serve.

Ahme hnat hin
Ginger beef

Serves 6 Cooking time 1 hour 10 minutes

2 onions	2 tablespoons oil
5 cloves garlic	3 lb (1.5 kg) steak (rump or
4 in (10 cm) fresh root ginger	sirloin)
2 teaspoons salt	1 can peeled tomatoes
1 teaspoon chilli powder	1 cup beef stock

Preparation
Chop the onions, garlic and ginger. Place in an electric blender
with the salt and chilli powder and a little of the oil. Blend to a
smooth paste. Cut the steak into bite-size pieces. Mix the meat
and paste together and leave to marinate for 4 hours.

Cooking
Heat the oil in a large deep pan and add the meat and marinade.
Fry until brown, then add the tomatoes and beef stock. Reduce
the heat, cover and simmer for about 1 hour or until the meat is
tender. Serve.

Ah mhae tha hin
Minced beef curry

Serves 6 Cooking time 25 minutes

2 onions	1 teaspoon powdered ginger
2 cloves garlic	2 lb (1 kg) minced beef
1 teaspoon salt	2 tablespoons soy sauce
1 teaspoon chilli powder	1 tablespoon water
½ teaspoon saffron	

Preparation Finely chop the onions. Mince the garlic.

Cooking
Heat the oil in a large heavy pan. Add the onions and garlic and
fry for 5 minutes. Sprinkle on the salt, chilli powder, saffron and
powdered ginger. Stir for 1 minute, then add the minced beef.
Continue to stir for 5 minutes, then pour in the soy sauce and 1
tablespoon of water. Continue to cook until the liquid has
evaporated, then serve.

Poultry

Kway swe
Chicken coconut curry

Serves 4 Cooking time 1 hour

1 2-lb (1-kg) chicken	2 fresh green chillies
1 teaspoon salt	2 fresh red chillies
1 teaspoon turmeric	3 eggs
2 onions	2 tablespoons oil
10 cloves garlic	1½ cups coconut milk (see page 105)
1 in (2.5 cm) fresh root ginger	½ teaspoon pepper

Preparation

Skin the chicken and cut into pieces. Sprinkle with the salt, place in a saucepan and cover with water. Add the turmeric. Finely chop the onion, crush and chop the garlic, grate the root ginger, chop the green chillies and then pound or blend them all together until you have a paste. Finely slice the red chillies and put to one side. Hardboil and finely chop the eggs. Put to one side.

Cooking

Put the saucepan containing the chicken over a moderate heat, cover and bring to the boil. Continue to boil until the meat starts to come off the bones. Remove the chicken, strain and retain the stock. Allow the chicken to slightly cool, then remove all the meat. Discard the bones. Heat the oil in a large heavy pan and gently fry the blended ingredients for 5 minutes. Remove from the heat and add the chicken meat. Return the pan to the heat and continue to fry until the chicken just starts to colour, then just cover with some of the retained stock. Add the coconut milk and leave to simmer until the sauce becomes thick. Season with the pepper and add the sliced red chillies. Serve immediately, garnished with the chopped hardboiled eggs.

Panthay kwowse
Burmese curried chicken

Serves 6 Cooking time 50 minutes

1 5-lb (2.25-kg) chicken	6 cloves garlic
3 onions	2 in (5 cm) fresh root ginger

2 eggs
6 spring onions
2 fresh red chillies
2 tablespoons cornflour
4 tablespoons oil
2 teaspoons turmeric

½ teaspoon ground cumin
1 teaspoon ground coriander
1 teaspoon garam masala
1 teaspoon chilli powder
4 cups coconut milk (see page 105)
2 teaspoons salt

Preparation

Disjoint the chicken and cut into small serving portions. Finely slice the onions. Crush and finely chop the garlic. Mince the ginger. Hardboil the eggs and slice into quarters. Chop the spring onions. Finely slice the red chillies. Blend the cornflour with a little water.

Cooking

Heat the oil in a large heavy pan. Toss in the onions, garlic, ginger, turmeric, cumin, coriander, garam masala and chilli powder. Fry together, stirring, for 5 minutes. Add the chicken pieces and continue to fry for 10 minutes. Pour in half the coconut milk and add the salt. Cover and simmer for 25 minutes or until the chicken is tender. Add the cornflour and water with the remaining coconut milk. Stir continuously until it is thick and is ready to serve. Transfer to a serving bowl and spread the quarters of hardboiled egg on top and sprinkle with the chopped spring onions and sliced red chillies. Serve at once.

Bhae tha-woon bai hin
Duck curry

Serves 6   Cooking time 1¼ hours

1 4-lb (2-kg) duck
10 onions
2 in (5 cm) fresh root ginger
10 cloves garlic
6 dried red chillies
1 bay leaf

3 tablespoons soy sauce
1 teaspoon turmeric
2 teaspoons salt
1 large green apple
6 whole black peppercorns
oil for frying

Preparation

Using a sharp knife, prick the skin of the duck all over. Cut 5 of the onions in quarters and place in an electric blender. Chop the ginger and the garlic and add to the onions. Toss in the dried

chillies and bay leaf and blend until you have a thick paste. Mix
together the soy sauce, turmeric and salt and put to one side.
Slice the remaining onions and the apple and also put to one side.
Preheat the oven to 450°F, 235°C or Gas Mark 8.

Cooking
Place the duck on a rack and put in the preheated oven for 20
minutes to allow some of the fat to melt and escape. Remove from
the oven, allow to drain thoroughly and cool. When cool enough
to handle, cut into serving portions. Rub each portion thoroughly
with the soy sauce mixture and leave for at least 2 hours. Pour the
oil into a large heavy pan and heat. Carefully add the blended
ingredients along with the 6 whole peppercorns. Fry for 1 or 2
minutes, then add the duck portions. Continue to fry until the
duck portions are brown, then pour in enough water to just cover
them. Allow to simmer for a further 45 minutes. When cooked,
place the duck portions on a hot serving plate, top with the sliced
apples and onions and pour over the cooking sauce.

Chet-glay hin
Chicken curry

Serves 6 Cooking time 1½ hours

1 4-lb (2-kg) chicken	1 in (2.5 cm) fresh root ginger
2 teaspoons turmeric	½ teaspoon chilli powder
3 teaspoons salt	1 tablespoon rice flour
8 onions	1 cup coconut milk (see page 105)
6 cloves garlic	3 tablespoons oil

Preparation
Disjoint the chicken and cut into serving portions. Rub all the
portions with the turmeric and the salt. Coarsely chop 6 of the
onions, then mince with the garlic and ginger. To the minced
ingredients, add the chilli powder. Slice the remaining onions.
Blend the rice flour and cream the coconut milk.

Cooking
Place the chicken portions into a saucepan and just cover with
hot water. Bring to the boil, reduce the heat and simmer for 20
minutes or until the chicken is tender enough to come away from

the bone easily. Strain and retain the cooking liquid for stock. When the chicken pieces are cool enough to handle, remove all the flesh from the bones. Take a large heavy frying pan and pour in the oil. Allow to get hot, then toss in the sliced onions and fry until just golden brown. Add the chicken and continue to fry until the chicken starts to brown. Add the minced ingredients and fry for 2 more minutes before pouring in 1 cup of the retained chicken stock. Reduce the heat and leave to simmer for 5 minutes. Pour in the coconut milk cream and stir. Continue to simmer for a further 10 minutes or until the sauce is thick, then serve.

Vegetables

Hin nu hwe
Fried spinach

Serves 6 Cooking time 12 minutes

2 lb (1 kg) spinach	2 teaspoons salt
1 onion	$\frac{1}{2}$ teaspoon chilli powder
2 cloves garlic	1 teaspoon turmeric
1 anchovy fillet	2 tablespoons water
4 tablespoons oil	

Preparation
Wash and drain the spinach, then shred it coarsely. Finely slice the onion. Cut the garlic into very thin slices. Mince the achovy fillet.

Cooking
Heat the oil in a large heavy pan. Add the onion and garlic. Fry for 1 minute, then add the salt, chilli powder, turmeric and the minced anchovy fillet. Continue to fry for 5 minutes. Add the shredded spinach and water. Cover, reduce the heat and cook for 5 minutes. Remove the cover, increase the heat and let the spinach start to dry out before serving.

Desserts

Sa nwin ma kin
Semolina pudding

Serves 6 Cooking time 1 hour

3 cups semolina
2 cups sugar
5 cups coconut milk (see page 105)
3 egg whites

4 oz (125 g) butter
1 cup raisins
1 tablespoon blanched slivered
 almonds .

Preparation

Mix together the semolina, sugar and coconut milk. Leave to
stand for 20 minutes. Beat the egg whites until stiff. Use a little of
the butter to grease a baking dish. Preheat the oven to 325°F,
165°C or Gas Mark 3.

Cooking

Place the semolina mixture in a saucepan, place over a moderate
heat and gently bring to the boil. Add the remaining butter and
stir continuously until the mixture becomes thick. Remove from
the heat and fold in the stiffly beaten egg whites and the raisins.
Pour into the buttered baking dish and sprinkle with the
blanched slivered almonds. Place in the preheated oven and bake
for 45 minutes. Leave to cool, then chill in the refrigerator before
turning out and serving.

Sri Lanka

Sri Lanka (or Ceylon as it was once known) has one of the most colourful cuisines in the world. True to the tradition of Asian cooking, its food is dazzling to the eye. Garnishes of flowers and fruit on a background of green banana leaves provide a kaleidoscope of texture and colour which make the meals mouthwatering. Local herbs and spices impregnate the dish not only with their pungent taste, but their colour. Many dishes have colour names: black curries, red curries, white curries. The black comes from the toasting of cumin, coriander, and fennel until they are dark brown; the red from pounded red chillies; and the white from creamy coconut milk.

In spite of the abundant wildlife roaming through the country's 25,000 square miles of woodlands (much of which would end up in the cooking pots in many countries!) Sri Lankans are largely vegetarians. Their staple diet relies on locally grown produce such as coconut, rice and fish.

Much of the food eaten today has been influenced by Dutch, Malay, Portuguese and Indian traders who left behind their culinary art for the locals to incorporate in their food. However, the ingredients that go into the *chatty* (clay cooking pot) have not changed in hundreds of years. Nor has the method of eating curries, rice, fiery-hot *sambals* and soups, which are all served at one time on banana leaves and eaten with fingers and the aid of hoppers. These are pancake-type breads made from fermented rice batter, crisp on the outside, spongy inside. The hopper is used to mop up the sauces and gravies which are difficult to pick up with one's fingers.

Seafood
Kakuluwo
Crab curry

Serves 6 Cooking time 1 hour 10 minutes

3 large uncooked crabs
4 onions
5 cloves garlic
2 in (5 cm) fresh root ginger
½ teaspoon fenugreek seeds
2 teaspoons turmeric
2 teaspoons chilli powder

1 teaspoon cumin seeds
4-in (10-cm) cinnamon stick
1 teaspoon salt
6 cups coconut milk (see page 105)
3 tablespoons desiccated coconut
1 tablespoon rice flour
juice of 2 lemons

Preparation
Wash the crabs thoroughly and cut them into serving portions. Remove all the inedible pieces. Crack the claws. Chop the onions and garlic. Grate the ginger.

Cooking
Toss the onions, garlic, ginger, fenugreek seeds, turmeric, chilli powder, cumin seeds, cinnamon stick and the salt into a large heavy saucepan or flameproof casserole. Add 4 cups of coconut

milk and place over a moderate heat. Bring to the boil, reduce the heat, cover and leave to simmer for 25 minutes. In the meantime, toast the desiccated coconut and the rice flour in a pan until they are just turning brown. Stir continuously otherwise they will easily burn. Add the crab pieces to the cooking sauce and simmer for a further 20 minutes. Make sure the crabs are submerged under the sauce all the time. Remove the crabs after the 20 minutes and place in a serving bowl in a warm oven. Put the browned desiccated coconut and rice flour into a blender with the remaining coconut milk and blend together for a few seconds. Pour into the curry sauce and add the lemon juice. Stir well and simmer for a further 10 minutes, then return the crabs to the pan. Stir and simmer for 5 more minutes, remove the cinnamon stick, then serve.

Isso thel dhala
Deep-fried prawns

Serves 4 Cooking time 5 minutes remove the cunnamon stick,

2 cloves garlic	2 teaspoons sugar
1 teaspoon ground coriander	1 teaspoon salt
1 teaspoon powder ginger	1 tablespoon vinegar
1 teaspoon turmeric	8 oz (250 g) green prawns
½ teaspoon chilli powder	oil for deep-frying

Preparation
Crush and finely chop the garlic. Peel and devein the prawns. Wash under cold running water and pat dry. Mix together the prawns, garlic, spices, sugar, salt and vinegar and leave to marinate for 4 hours. Drain thoroughly and put out to dry. Before cooking, the prawns must be free of moisture. Leave them in the sun or on a rack in a breezy area of your kitchen.

Cooking
Heat the oil in a deep pan. Add the prawns and deep-fry until golden brown. Drain and serve immediately.

Ambul thiyal
Sour fish curry

Serves 6 Cooking time 20 minutes

1 lb (500 g) white fish fillets (cod, bream, snapper)	1 teaspoon salt
1 onion	2-in (5-cm) cinnamon stick
3 cloves garlic	¼ teaspoon fenugreek seeds
2 in (5 cm) fresh root ginger	½ teaspoon freshly ground black pepper
peel of ¼ lemon	½ teaspoon chilli powder
1 tablespoon lemon juice	1½ cups water
2 teaspoons vinegar	2 tablespoons oil

Preparation
Wash the fish under cold running water, drain and pat dry. Cut into medium-sized serving portions. Finely chop the onion. Crush and chop the garlic. Grate the ginger. Grate the lemon peel.

Cooking
Put all the ingredients apart from the fish into a large pan and bring to the boil. Reduce the heat and add the fish. Simmer, uncovered, until the fish is cooked and the gravy is nice and thick. To serve, put the pieces of fish on to a hot serving dish, remove the cinnamon stick and pour the gravy over the fish.

Meat

Kuruma iraichchi
Dry fried beef curry

Serves 6 Cooking time 1 hour

2 lb (1 kg) braising steak	peel of ½ lemon
2 onions	1 teaspoon turmeric
8 cloves garlic	3 tablespoons ground coriander
2 in (5 cm) fresh root ginger	juice of ½ lemon
2 fresh green chillies	2 teaspoons brown sugar
2 cups coconut milk (see page 105)	

Preparation
Cut the meat into bite-size pieces. Cut the onions in quarters and place in an electric blender. Add the garlic, ginger, green chillies

and a little of the coconut milk. Blend until you have a smooth paste. Grate the lemon peel.

Cooking

Pour the paste into a heavy pan and add the remaining coconut milk, meat, turmeric, ground coriander and the grated lemon peel. Place over a moderate heat and bring to the boil. Reduce the heat and continue to simmer for 30 minutes. Add the lemon juice, stir well and continue to simmer until the sauce becomes thick. When this happens, reduce the heat even further and continue to stir to prevent burning. Add the sugar and continue to stir until the sauce is completely dried out and has become dark brown. Serve.

Harak mas
Beef curry

Serves 4 Cooking time 1 hour

1 lb (500 g) braising steak	6 cups water
4 cloves garlic	10 black peppercorns
2 in (5 cm) fresh root ginger	1 small can peeled tomatoes
6 onions	4-in (10-cm) cinnamon stick
½ teaspoon turmeric	1 tablespoon coriander
½ teaspoon chilli powder	1 bay leaf
1 cup milk	1 tablespoon oil

Preparation

Cut the meat into bite-size pieces. Crush and chop the garlic. Grate the ginger. Coarsely chop half the onions and finely slice the remaining onions. Blend together the turmeric, chilli powder and milk and put to one side.

Cooking

Put the 6 cups of water in a pan and add the peppercorns, the coarsely chopped onions, the can of peeled tomatoes, including the juice, the cinammon stick (which can be broken into 2 or 3 pieces), the coriander, garlic, grated ginger, bay leaf and finally the meat. Place over a moderate heat and bring to the boil. Reduce the heat and simmer until the meat is tender. Add the milk, chilli and turmeric mixture. Stir well and continue to simmer for a further 5 minutes. In the meantime, heat the oil in a heavy pan and fry the remaining sliced onions until they are just golden brown. Drain them, add to the pan and mix thoroughly. Continue to simmer for a further 10 minutes, then remove the cinnamon sticks and serve.

Ooroomas badun
Curried pork

Serves 6 Cooking time 1¾ hours

1½ lb (750 g) pork steaks	1 teaspoon turmeric
6 fresh red chillies	½ teaspoon cinnamon powder
6 cloves garlic	½ teaspoon ground cloves
2 in (5 cm) fresh root ginger	1 tablespoon vinegar
1 teaspoon cumin seeds	2 onions
6 black peppercorns	1 tablespoon oil

Preparation
Trim away the excess fat from the pork and cut into bite-size pieces. Place the red chillies, garlic, ginger, cumin seeds, peppercorns, turmeric, cinnamon, ground cloves and vinegar into an electric blender. Blend until you have a smooth paste. Finely chop the onions.

Cooking
Place the pork in a heavy saucepan and just cover with hot water. Place over a moderate heat, bring to the boil and boil for 1 hour. Remove and drain thoroughly. Heat the oil in a large heavy pan and toss in the drained pork pieces. Fry until brown. Remove the pork and drain off the excess fat and oil, leaving just enough to fry the onions until they are golden brown. Now return the pork to the pan. Pour in the blended paste and mix all together thoroughly. Simmer over a low heat for about 20 minutes, then serve.

Peegodu
Liver curry

Serves 6 Cooking time 45 minutes

1½ lb (750 g) calves liver	3 tablespoons oil
2 onions	½ teaspoon ground cloves
4 cloves garlic	1 teaspoon cinnamon powder
2 in (5 cm) fresh root ginger	1 teaspoon freshy ground black
peel of ¼ lemon	pepper
8 black peppercorns	4 tablespoons wine vinegar
2 teaspoons salt	2½ cups coconut milk (see page 105)

Preparation
Wash the liver under cold running water and pat dry. Cut into 3 or 4 thick slices. Finely chop the onions. Crush and chop the garlic. Finely chop the ginger and the lemon peel.

Cooking
Place the liver in a large heavy saucepan and cover with water. Add the peppercorns and salt and place over a moderate heat. Bring gently to the boil and cook for about 20 minutes or until the liver is firm. Remove and drain. Leave to cool slightly, then cut into small thin slices. Heat the oil in a large heavy pan and add the onion, garlic and ginger. Fry until the onions become transparent, then add the sliced liver. Add the lemon peel, cloves, cinnamon, freshly ground black pepper, vinegar and coconut milk to the pan. Cook, uncovered, over a low heat until you have a thick gravy, then serve.

Poultry

Kukul mas
Chicken curry

Serves 6 Cooking time 1¼ hours

1 3½-lb (1.75-kg) chicken	½ teaspoon ground cumin
2 onions	2 teaspoons ground coriander
2 in (5 cm) fresh root ginger	½ teaspoon turmeric
4 cloves garlic	2 cups chicken stock
2 tablespoons oil	3 cups coconut milk (see page 105)
2-in (5-cm) cinnamon stick	juice of ½ lemon
6 cloves	1 teaspoon salt
4 cardamom pods	2 sprigs parsley
½ teaspoon chilli powder	

Preparation
Cut the chicken into serving pieces. Finely slice the onions. Mince the garlic and ginger.

Cooking
Heat the oil in a heavy pan and fry the chicken pieces with the cinnamon stick, cloves and cardamom pods. When the chicken is brown, reduce the heat and add the onions, garlic and ginger. Continue to fry until the onions become transparent. Add the chilli powder, cumin, coriander, turmeric and the chicken stock. Stir well and bring to the boil. Reduce the heat, cover and leave to simmer for 30 minutes. Pour in the coconut milk and add the lemon juice and salt. Stir and simmer for 5 minutes, then pour into a serving bowl. As you pour, remove the cloves, cardamom pods and cinnamon stick. Garnish with the parsley.

Thara padre
Padre's duck curry

Serves 6 Cooking time 1 hour

2 3½-lb (1.75-kg) ducks	1 in (2.5 cm) cinnamon stick
2 onions	3½ cups coconut milk (see page 105)
8 cloves garlic	2 teaspoons salt
2 in (5 cm) fresh root ginger	1 tablespoon wine vinegar
peel of ¼ lemon	2 teaspoons ground coriander

½ teaspoon ground cumin	1 teaspoon chilli powder
½ teaspoon fennel seeds	2 tablespoons oil
½ teaspoon fenugreek seeds	2 tablespoons whisky
½ teaspoon ground cloves	1 tablespoon sugar
½ teaspoon ground cardamom	

Preparation

Cut the ducks into serving portions. Finely chop the onions. Crush and chop the garlic. Grate the ginger. Finely chop the lemon peel.

Cooking

Put the duck pieces in a very large heavy saucepan and add the onions, garlic, ginger, lemon peel, cinnamon, coconut milk, salt, vinegar, coriander, cumin, fennel, fenugreek, cloves, cardamom and chilli powder. Place over a moderate heat and simmer, covered, until the duck is tender. Remove the duck pieces and drain. Retain the gravy. Heat the oil in a large heavy pan. Add the duck pieces and fry for 2 minutes. Pour in the gravy and add the whisky and sugar. Stir well and simmer for 10 minutes, then serve.

Vegetables and rice

Brinjals
Baked aubergines

Serves 6 Cooking time 45 minutes

1 clove garlic	2 teaspoons salt
2 large aubergines	1 teaspoon freshy ground black pepper
1 cup dry breadcrumbs	2 onions
½ teaspoon powdered ginger	3 sprigs parsley
1 teaspoon turmeric	6 tablespoons butter

Preparation

Cut the garlic in half and rub the inside of a deep casserole with it. Peel and slice the aubergines lengthwise into thin slices. Place several slices on the bottom of the casserole. Mix together the breadcrumbs, ginger, turmeric, salt and freshly ground black pepper. Finely chop the onions and the parsley and add to the breadcrumb mixture. Sprinkle some of the mixture on top of the first layer of aubergine. Arrange a second layer and sprinkle again. Continue in this fashion until you use all the aubergine and the breadcrumb mixture. Melt the butter and pour over the top. Preheat your oven to 350°F, 175°C or Gas Mark 4.

Cooking
Place the casserole in the preheated oven and bake for 45 minutes, then serve.

Mallung
Green vegetables and coconut

Serves 6 Cooking time 12 minutes

1 lb (500 g) mixed green veget- | 3 oz (90 g) desiccated coconut
ables (whatever is in season – | ½ teaspoon saffron
beans, spinach, cabbage, etc.) | 2 tablespoons water
4 fresh green chillies | 1 tablespoon lemon juice
1 onion | 1 teaspoon salt

Preparation
Wash all the vegetables and coarsely shred them. Finely slice the green chillies. Finely slice the onion.

Cooking
Heat the oil in a large heavy pan. Add the sliced chillies and fry for 5 minutes. Pour off most of the oil and then add the shredded vegetables, coconut, saffron and the 2 tablespoons of water. Cover and cook for 5 minutes. Add the lemon juice and salt, stir and cook, uncovered, for 2 minutes. Serve at once.

Elolu kiri hodhi
Mixed vegetable curry

Serves 6 Cooking time depends on vegetables used

1 onion | 4 cups coconut milk (see page 105)
2 cloves garlic | 1 teaspoon turmeric
2 fresh green chillies | 1 teaspoon cinnamon powder
2 in (5 cm) fresh root ginger | 2 teaspoons salt
peel of ¼ lemon |
1½ lb (750 g) mixed fresh |
vegetables – beans, potatoes, |
carrots, courgettes, etc. |

Preparation

Finely chop the onion. Crush and chop the garlic. Slice the green chillies. Grate the ginger and the lemon peel. Slice all the vegetables.

Cooking

Put 3 cups of the coconut milk into a large saucepan and add the onions, chillies, ginger, lemon peel, turmeric and cinnamon. Place over a moderate heat and bring gently to the boil. Reduce the heat and leave, uncovered, to simmer for 10 minutes. Start to add the vegetables. Put those that require more cooking in first and add the rest according to the time required. Let them all cook until they are just tender, then add the remaining coconut milk and the salt. Bring to the boil and cook for a further 5 minutes, then serve.

Kaha bath
Golden rice

Serves 6 Cooking time 30 minutes

3 cups long-grain rice	15 black peppercorns
2 onions	2 teaspoons turmeric
12 cardamom pods	3 teaspoons salt
3 tablespoon oil	5 cups coconut milk (see page 105)
6 cloves	

Preparation

Wash the rice under cold running water until the water passing through runs clear. Drain thoroughly. Finely slice the onions. Bruise the cardamom pods.

Cooking

Heat the oil in a large heavy saucepan and add the onions. Fry until they are golden brown. Toss in the cloves, peppercorns, turmeric and salt. Stir well, then add the rice and fry. Stir continuously until all the rice is coated with the turmeric and oil. Pour in the coconut milk and bring slowly to the boil. Reduce the heat, cover and leave to simmer for 20 minutes. Do not lift the lid during this period. When the rice is cooked, remove the whole spices and serve.

Bread

Appe
Hoppers

Makes about 12 Cooking time 30 minutes

1 teaspoon dried yeast	1 teaspoon salt
½ cup warm water	2½ cups desiccated coconut
1½ teaspoons sugar	2½ cups hot milk
1½ cups ground rice	2 cups hot water
1½ cups plain flour	

Preparation

Mix together the yeast, warm water and sugar. Leave for 10 minutes. The yeast should bubble and froth. Mix together the ground rice, flour and salt in a large bowl. Make some coconut milk by blending the hot milk and the coconut together and straining the liquid. Add this liquid to the yeast. Return the damp coconut to the blender and add the hot water. Blend and strain and put to one side.

Pour the yeast and coconut milk mixture into the dry ingredients and mix well to form a smooth thick batter. Place in a warm, turned-off oven for 1 hour, or any other suitable warm place so that the yeast can work and the batter doubles in size. By now, the batter should be of a thick pouring consistency. Add a little of the second batch of coconut milk to ensure that it is.

Cooking

Heat a large heavy pan over a low heat. Smear the pan with a little oil on a piece of kitchen paper. Pour in a ladle of batter and swirl it round to give a thin even coating. Cover the pan and cook for 5 minutes – do not lift the lid until the 5 minutes are up. When the top edges just start to turn brown, it is ready. Remove and repeat the process with the rest of the batter. Serve warm with curries.

Korea

Korea lies right between China and Japan and her cuisine is influenced by both. The cooking of Korea is far more involved than that of Japan but nowhere as sophisticated as China. Dishes are not as rich and varied as those eaten in China but are spicier than either China or Japan. A Korean cook thinks nothing of adding heaped spoons of chilli to give a dish the characteristic pungency that her guests will enjoy. Korean food is robust, wholesome and warming – which is needed in a country with such a severely cold climate.

The strong flavours that characterise Korean cooking are usually obtained by combining a number of spices, such as pepper, chillies, garlic and sesame, accompanied by the ever present *kim chi*. Made from mixed vegetables, cabbage, turnip, white radish, seasoned with seafood, salt, garlic and chilli, *kim chi* can be mild, but in most cases is best avoided as it is extremely strong in smell, flavour and chilli. All the ingredients are washed and chopped and placed in large urns which are buried underground for fermentation. *Kim chi* is normally consumed in large quantities in the winter as a protein supplement, when the fermentation period lasts for up to six months. I've included my version of *kim chi* – a much milder and less pungent pickle.

Kim chi is unique, and so is the table cooking found in Korea. Two styles of cooking predominate even though many others are found in isolated communities where traditions have lasted. Firstly, *shinsulro*, which is a thick soupy stew, full of vegetables, meat and seafood in a seaweed-based soup. There is no need to try and buy the right cooking pot – use a metal fondue pot, it works just as well. Neither is there a need to try and buy a *bulgogi*, as you can plug in an electric fry pan and place it in the centre of the table to give you excellent results. This form of cooking is found in both China and Japan as well as Korea and is supposed to have originated in the days of Genghis Khan in northern China. Genghis Khan's warriors wore metal hats which were placed on charcoal fires and heated. Meat and vegetables were placed on the hats and cooked. Today, dome-shaped barbecue plates are still used in all three countries and are a basic utensil to be found in all Korean kitchens.

Starters and snacks

Mandoo
Dumplings

Serves 6 Cooking time 25 minutes

3 cups plain flour	2 spring onions
1 teaspoon salt	2 sprigs watercress
1 cup water	2 tablespoons soy sauce
4 oz (125 g) cold roast pork	1 teaspoon chilli powder
½ cup bean sprouts (fresh or canned)	oil for frying

Preparation
Sift the flour into a bowl. Add the salt and pour in the water. Mix until you have a stiff dough. Knead for a few minutes and then leave for 30 minutes. In the meantime, dice the pork, chop the bean sprouts, the spring onions and watercress. Mix all together and add the soy sauce and chilli powder

Roll the dough out, as thin as possible, on to a floured surface. Cut into pieces about 3 in by 2 in (7.5 cm by 5 cm). Place a small amount of the mixed vegetables and meat into the centre of each piece of dough. Fold over the dough and seal with a little water. Press the edges firmly together.

Cooking
Bring a large saucepan of water to the boil and put in the dumplings. Boil for 10 minutes. Drain thoroughly. Heat the oil in a large pan and add the dumplings. Fry until they are just brown, drain on kitchen paper and serve.

Soups

Mandoo kuk
Dumpling soup

Serves 6 Cooking time 3¼ hours

24 mandoo dumplings (see above)	2 in (5 cm) fresh root ginger
4 lb (2 kg) beef bones	2 teaspoons salt
2 lb (1 kg) shin beef	2 tablespoons soy sauce

Preparation

Make the mandoo dumplings, but do not boil or fry them. Crush the ginger.

Cooking

Put the bones, beef and the ginger into a large saucepan. Cover with water and season with the salt. Bring to the boil, reduce the heat and simmer for 3 hours. Remove the scum occasionally. Strain and place 9 cups of the stock into a second smaller saucepan. Add the soy sauce and dumplings. Place over a moderate heat and simmer for 10 minutes, then serve.

Naig kuk
Cold cucumber soup

Serves 6

1 large cucumber
2 spring onions
2 tablespoons soy sauce
2 tablespoons wine vinegar
1 teaspoon sugar

2 teaspoons sesame sauce (see page 191)
1 teaspoon chilli powder
6 cups chilled chicken stock

Preparation

Slice the cucumber very thinly. Chop the spring onions and mix with the soy sauce, vinegar, sugar, sesame sauce and chilli powder. Put the cucumber into this mixture and leave to marinate for at least 30 minutes. Add the chicken stock and place in a refrigerator for at least 2 hours before serving.

Seafood
Gun saen-gsun
Grilled sardines

Serves 6 Cooking time 20 minutes

6 medium sardines
2 in (5 cm) fresh root ginger
2 cloves garlic
3 tablespoons sesame seeds

2 teaspoons chilli powder
2 teaspoons sugar
3 tablespoons soy sauce
1 tablespoon oil

Preparation

Clean the fish thoroughly and remove the heads. Grate the ginger. Crush and chop the garlic. Toast the sesame seeds in a dry pan until they start to pop and brown, then put into a blender and grind to a powder. Add the garlic, ginger, chilli powder, sugar, soy sauce and oil. Blend until you have a smooth sauce. Cover each fish with the sauce and leave for 5 minutes

Cooking

Place the fish under a hot grill and cook, basting from time to time with the sauce. Turn the fish over to grill the other side and baste. When the fish is cooked through, serve.

Meat
Kah-ri kui
Grilled spareribs

Serves 4 Cooking time 12 minutes

3 lb (1½ kg) pork spareribs	8 tablespoon soy sauce
2 cloves garlic	3 tablespoons sugar
6 spring onions	4 tablespoons sesame seeds
2 tablespoons cornflour	

Preparation

Separate the ribs. Crush and finely chop the garlic. Finely chop the spring onions. Make a marinade by mixing together the cornflour, soy sauce, sugar and sesame seeds. Add the garlic and spring onions and stir well. Place the spareribs in a flat deep dish and pour over the marinade mixture. Leave to marinate for 2 hours.

Cooking

Drain and retain the marinade. Place the spareribs on a grill tray and place under a hot grill. Cook for 5 to 6 minutes. Turn the spareribs over, baste with the retained marinade and cook for a further 5 minutes. Serve at once.

Shinsulro
Hot pot

Serves 4 Cooking time at table

8 oz (250 g) fillet steak	½ cup flour
8 oz (250 g) calves liver	3 tablespoons oil
8 oz (250 g) white fish fillets	½ cup walnuts
1 large onion	½ cup almonds
4 spring onions	8 cups beef stock
1 carrot	4 tablespoons sesame sauce (see
3 eggs	page 191)

Preparation

Cut the steak into wafer-thin slices. Either have your butcher do this or freeze the meat and slice while frozen. Slice the liver in a similar way. Cut the fish into bite-size pieces, removing any bones or skin. Coarsely slice the onion. Cut the spring onions in half. Peel and slice the carrot into thin strips. Beat one of the eggs and dip the liver and fish into it and then into the flour. Put to one side. Beat the remaining eggs.

Heat 2 tablespoons of the oil in a pan and fry the fish first and then the liver until they are just cooked. Put to one side. Clean out the pan, add the remaining oil and pour in the beaten eggs. Allow to set, remove and cut in thin strips.

Take a large fondue pot and place the thin slices of steak on the bottom. Put the sliced onions on top, then the liver and fish. On top of that, place the spring onions, carrots and omelette strips. Finally top with the walnuts and almonds.

Cooking

Heat the beef stock and when hot, carefully pour into the fondue. Place the fondue pot over the table fire and allow to simmer for a few minutes. Guest help themselves with chopsticks to the pieces and dip them in the sesame sauce.

Beef bulgagi
Korean beef barbecue

Serves 4 Cooking time at table

2 lb (1 kg) lean beef steak (rump, sirloin)	4 tablespoons sesame seeds
2 spring onions	6 tablespoons soy sauce
6 cloves garlic	1 teaspoon freshly ground pepper
2 in (5 cm) fresh root ginger	4 tablespoons oil

Preparation
Cut the meat into small thin slices. Coarsely chop the spring onions, garlic and the ginger, then mince. Pound the sesame seeds until very fine. Mix together the minced ingredients with the pounded sesame seeds and add the soy sauce. Add the pepper and oil and stir well before tossing in the meat and leaving it to marinate for 10 minutes.

Cooking
Plug in an electric frying pan and place it in the centre of the table. Allow to get hot, then each guest cooks his own meat. Alternatively it may be cooked on a solid plate outdoor barbecue.

Serve with *chicken bulgagi* (see page 188), salads, *kim chi* (see page 190), and dips of soy sauce and chilli sauce.

Koon ko ki
Fried steak

Serves 4 Cooking time 10 minutes

2 lb (1 kg) rump steak	7 tablespoons sesame sauce (see page 191)
2 cloves garlic	3 teaspoons cornflour
2 spring onions	
2 tablespoons oil	

Preparation
Cut the steak into 4 pieces. Trim away any excess fat. Mince the garlic and spring onions. Mix together the sesame sauce, garlic and spring onions. Spread over the steaks and leave to marinate for 2 hours. Drain the marinade and put into a small saucepan.

Cooking

Heat the oil in a large heavy pan. Toss in the steaks and fry until cooked to your requirements. Place the saucepan containing the marinade over a low heat and simmer. Add the cornflour mixed with a little water to thicken. Serve the steaks and pour over the sauce.

Poultry

Chicken bulgagi
Chicken barbecue

Serves 4 Cooking time at table

2 lb (1 kg) chicken breasts	4 tablespoon sesame seeds
3 tablespoons caster sugar	½ teaspoon freshly ground pepper
12 spring onions	3 tablespoons oil
2 in (5 cm) fresh root ginger	3 tablespoons soy sauce
12 cloves garlic	

Preparation

Remove the flesh from the chicken breasts and cut the meat into thin slices. Sprinkle with the caster sugar. Coarsely chop the onions, ginger and garlic, then finely mince. Pound the sesame seeds, then add the onions, ginger, garlic, oil and soy sauce. Mix thoroughly and toss in the slices of chicken. Leave to marinate for 15 minutes.

Cooking

Plug in an electric frying pan and place it in the centre of the table. Allow to get hot, then each guest cooks his own meat. Alternatively it may be cooked on a solid plate outdoor barbecue.

Serve with *beef bulgagi* (see page 187), salads, *kim chi* (see page 190), and dips of soy sauce and chilli sauce.

Sow see gai
Korean chicken salad

Serves 6 Cooking time 20 minutes

1 4-lb (2-kg) chicken	3 tablespoons soy sauce
4 tablespoons sherry	2 teaspoons sugar

½ teaspoon chilli powder
½ teaspoon powdered ginger
4 tablespoons blanched almonds
1 medium lettuce
2 stalks celery

1 cup bean sprouts (fresh or canned)
3 tablespoons sesame seeds
3 tablespoons oil

Preparation

Disjoint the chicken. Remove all the skin. Cut all the meat from the bone and chop into bite-size pieces. Make a mixture of the sherry, soy sauce, sugar, chilli powder and powdered ginger. Mix well and add the chicken pieces. Leave to marinate for 2 hours. In the meantime, chop the almonds, shred the lettuce and dice the celery. Mix them all together in a salad bowl and add the bean sprouts and sesame seeds. Drain the chicken from the marinade.

Cooking

Heat the oil in a frying pan. Toss in the chicken pieces and fry until brown. Cover and cook for a further 10 minutes until the chicken is tender. Remove with a slotted spoon, drain, cool and add to the salad. Serve with an oil and vinegar dressing.

Dak jim
Stewed chicken

Serves 6 Cooking time 1 hour

6 cloves garlic
3 spring onions
1 4-lb (2-kg) chicken
2 tablespoons soy sauce
2 tablespoons oil

2 tablespoons sesame sauce (see page 191)
1 teaspoon chilli powder
½ teaspoon salt

Preparation

Crush and chop the garlic. Finely chop the spring onions. Disjoint the chicken and cut into serving portions. Put all the ingredients into a large deep pan. Cover and leave for 3 hours.

Cooking

Place the pan over a moderate heat and cook until the chicken is tender, about 1 hour. Serve.

Rice

Kak pab
Nutty rice

Serves 6 Cooking time 20 minutes

1½ cups long-grain rice	½ cup walnuts
2½ cups water	1 tablespoon oil
1 teaspoon salt	3 tablespoons honey
½ cup blanched almonds	2 tablespoons soy sauce

Preparation
Wash the rice under cold running water until the water runs clear. Put in a saucepan and add the water and salt. Chop the almonds and walnuts.

Cooking
Cover the saucepan, bring to the boil and cook for 20 minutes. Heat the oil in a pan and lightly brown the nuts. When the rice is cooked, drain and add the nuts, honey and soy sauce. Mix together and serve.

Pickles and sauces

Kim chi
Radish pickle

Serves 6-12

1 lb (500 g) radishes	1 in (2.5 cm) fresh root ginger
4 oz (125 g) watercress	2 teaspoons chilli powder
2 small onions	2 teaspoons salt
8 cloves garlic	3 cups water

Preparation
Peel and chop the radishes. Rinse and chop the watercress. Mince the onions, garlic and ginger. Mix together the radishes, watercress, onions, garlic and ginger and add the chilli powder and 1 teaspoon of salt. Spoon into a large jar. Boil the 3 cups of water and dissolve the remaining salt in it. Leave to cool, then pour over the vegetables. Seal the jar and leave for 6 or 7 days before using.

Cho kanjang
Sesame sauce

1 cup sesame seeds	5 tablespoons vinegar
2 tablespoons sugar	9 tablespoons soy sauce

Preparation

Toast the sesame seeds in a dry pan until they start to pop and become golden brown. Pour into an electric blender and blend to a powder. Add the sugar, vinegar and soy sauce and blend until the sauce is smooth. Put into a bottle and store.

Weights and measures

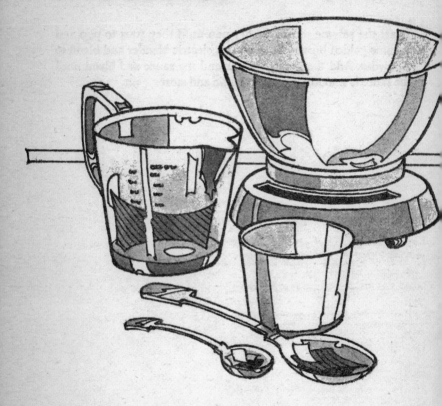

The weights and measures in this book are designed for both Avoirdupois and Metric, i.e. Avoirdupois 3 lb,   Metric 1.5 kg.

All other measurements are in metric cups, tablespoons and teaspoons. The metric measuring cup specified has a capacity of 250 millilitres (250 ml).

¼ metric cup	=	60 ml	1 metric cup	=	250 ml	= .25 litre
½ metric cup	=	125 ml	2 metric cups	=	500 ml	= .5 litre
¾ metric cup	=	185 ml	3 metric cups	=	750 ml	= .75 litre
			4 metric cups	=	1000 ml	= 1 litre

The standard teaspoon and tablespoon have the same capacity as the metric teaspoon and tablespoon.

1 metric teaspoon =   5 ml = 1 standard teaspoon
1 metric tablespoon = 20 ml = 1 standard tablespoon

Weight Equivalents

Imperial	Metric	Imperial	Metric
½ oz	15 g	11 oz	345 g
1 oz	30 g	12 oz (¾ lb)	375 g
2 oz	60 g	13 oz	410 g
3 oz	90 g	14 oz	440 g
4 oz (¼ lb)	125 g	15 oz	470 g
5 oz	155 g	16 oz (1 lb)	500 g (0.5 kg)
6 oz	185 g	24 oz (1½ lb)	750 g
7 oz	220 g	32 oz (2 lb)	1000 g (1 kg)
8 oz (½ lb)	250 g	3 lb	1500 g (1.5 kg)
9 oz	280 g	4 lb	2000 g (2 kg)
10 oz	315 g		

Liquid Equivalents

Imperial		Metric	
Liquid measures	Cup measures	Cup measures	Liquid measures
1 fl oz			30 ml
2 fl oz	⅓ cup	¼ cup	60 ml
3 fl oz			100 ml
4 fl oz		½ cup	125 ml
5 fl oz (¼ pint)		½ cup	150 ml
6 fl oz		¾ cup	
8 fl oz		1 cup	250 ml
10 fl oz (½ pint)		1¼ cups	
16 fl oz		2 cups	500 ml
20 fl oz (1 pint)		2½ cups	

Glossary

Almonds have been substituted in many cases for candlenuts and macadamia nuts which are not always obtainable. Brazil nuts can also be used as an alternative.

Bamboo shoots the tender new growth of bamboo sold in cans. Must be drained before use. Can be stored in fresh water in the refrigerator.

Bean curd tofu in Japan, made from soy beans. Is available fresh or canned.

Bean sprouts mung beans which have just sprouted. Available fresh or canned. Fresh are by far the best and can be replaced by very thinly sliced celery.

Cardamom the second most expensive spice in the world. Grown in India and Sri Lanka. They are small black seeds in a white or green pod. Can be purchased ground, as seeds or whole pods. The pods are sometimes bruised and added whole to a dish.

Cashew nuts a small sweet kidney-shaped nut. Readily available.

Chilli powder made from grinding red chillies.

Chilli sauce made from chillies, salt and vinegar. Very hot.

Chillies fresh green – the seeds are the hottest part and are usually removed.

fresh red – used for flavour and garnishing.

dried – can be crushed and used for flavouring.

If one particular type of chilli is specified and is unavailable, use one of the others. But be careful to taste and check that it is the required flavour and not too hot.

Cinnamon use cinnamon sticks and grind them yourself as required to obtain cinnamon powder, as prepacked powder tends to lose its flavour.

Coconut milk see recipe page 105. In the East the fresh flesh is grated and the milk extracted. It is not the liquid found in the centre of each coconut.

Coriander ground coriander seeds are the main ingredient in curry powders. It is a member of the parsley family and the fresh leaves are used for flavouring and garnishing dishes. Parsley is a good substitute. It is also called Chinese parsley. It is easily grown at home from the seeds.

Courgettes (French); Zucchini (Italian).

Cumin or cummin also essential in the preparation of curries and curry powder. Available as seed and ground.

Curry powder the anglicised version of 'daily ground mixed spices' for the preparation of curries. Never used in the East.

Dill similar in appearance to fennel but with a particular and different flavour.

Fennel available in ground and seed form. Invaluable in Sri Lankan dishes. Sometimes called sweet cumin.

Fenugreek a bitter seed used in curries in small quantities.

Fish sauce used in varying styles throughout Asia. Available under many names: *ngan-pya-ye* (Burmese); *nam pla* (Thai) and *nuoc mam* (Vietnamese). A recipe for *nuoc mam* appears on page 155 and this can be used for all recipes that require fish sauce.

Five-spice powder Chinese, a combination of Szechuan pepper, ground cloves, cinnamon, fennel and star anise.

Garam masala a mixture of ground spices. Can be purchased prepared.

Ginger fresh root ginger is essential in Asian cooking. Powdered ginger should not be used as a substitute.

Hoisin sauce a thick, brown, sweet sauce made from soy beans, garlic and spices. Available in bottles and cans.

Lemon grass used fresh in curries. Dried, requires about ten times the quantity. Thinly peeled lemon peel cut into thin strips can be substituted.

Mace the dried outer lacy case of the nutmeg. Similar in flavour to nutmeg but more delicate.

Mint used fresh as a flavour in curries and in sambals. Ideal for garnishing Asian food.

Mushrooms fresh mushrooms have been included in most recipes that require mushrooms. Dried Chinese and Japanese mushrooms can be substituted in the appropriate dishes. Dried mushrooms should be soaked in hot water for a few minutes, squeezed and sliced.

Mustard seeds the black mustard seeds are used in Asian cooking. These can be replaced by brown but never white.

Noodles called cellophane noodles or Japanese harusame – these are thin and transparent.
Vermicelli or somen are very thin, white noodles.

Nutmeg used as a sweet spice. Use sparingly. Available whole or ground. Whole nuts must be finely grated before use.

Oyster sauce a Chinese sauce made from oysters, soy sauce and salt. Adds a delicate flavour to all foods.

Paprika used in Asian cooking to give a dish a lusty red colouring. A mild, sweet spice made from ground dried paprika peppers, a member of the capsicum family.

Pepper freshly ground black peppercorns are used where required. Pepper or white pepper is used in other dishes.

Peppers red and green, also known as capsicum. These are large, mild peppers, used as a vegetable and garnish. The seeds and white pith inside should be removed before using.

Plum sauce a Chinese, sweet and spicy sauce made from plums, chillies and spices.

Poppy seeds always ground to a powder before being used as a thickening agent in curries and gravies.

Rice ground – used in batters, this gives a nice texture as it is more granular than rice flour.

Saffron this is the world's most expensive spice. Made from the dried stamens of millions of crocuses. It is available in threads or in a powder.

Sesame seeds used in Japanese, Chinese and particularly in Korean cooking. Available as whole white or black seeds. White is the most commonly used.

Snow peas mange tout is the French name for these peas. The pods and peas are cooked for 1 or 2 minutes and the pods eaten as well as the peas.

Soy sauce You cannot start to cook Asian food without soy sauce.

Spring onions also known incorrectly as shallots in Australia and scallions in the USA. The slender white and green leaves are chopped, shredded, minced and sliced in many Asian dishes.

Spring roll wrappers available in packets, frozen.

Star anise a Chinese spice shaped like a star with eight points.

Sugar demerera – use raw or brown.

Tamarind a pulpy acid-tasting fruit from which the pulp is removed and dried. To get tamarind liquid, a small piece of dried pulp is soaked in water. Lemon juice is a good substitute.

Turmeric a member of the ginger family. Often called Indian saffron, there is no substitute. The orange-yellow colouring is the mainstay of curry powders.

Yoghurt always use plain, unflavoured yoghurt, preferably goat's milk yoghurt.

Index